Paul Richards, *Ebola: How a People's Science Helped End an Epidemic*

Louisa Lombard, *State of Rebellion: Violence and Intervention in the Central African Republic*

Forthcoming titles

Odd-Helge Fjelstad, Wilson Prichard, Mick Moore, *Taxing Africa*

Celeste Hicks, *The Trial of Hissène Habré*

Hilary Matfess, *Women and the War on Boko Haram: Wives, Weapons, Witnesses*

Published by Zed Books and the IAI with the support of the following organizations:

The principal aim of the **International African Institute** is to promote scholarly understanding of Africa, notably its changing societies, cultures and languages. Founded in 1926 and based in London, it supports a range of seminars and publications including the journal Africa.
www.internationalafricaninstitute.org

Now more than a hundred years old, the **Royal African Society** today is Britain's leading organization promoting Africa's cause. Through its journal, African Affairs, and by organizing meetings, discussions and other activities, the society strengthens links between Africa and Britain and encourages understanding of Africa and its relations with the rest of the world.
www.royalafricansociety.org

The **World Peace Foundation**, founded in 1910, is located at the Fletcher School, Tufts University. The Foundation's mission is to promote innovative research and teaching, believing that these are critical to the challenges of making peace around the world, and should go hand in hand with advocacy and practical engagement with the toughest issues. Its central theme is 'reinventing peace' for the twenty-first century.
www.worldpeacefoundation.org

About the author

Kris Berwouts is an independent analyst and acknowledged expert on the Democratic Republic of Congo. Until 2012, he was the director of EurAc, the European NGO network for advocacy on Central Africa. He has worked with different bilateral and multilateral partners of the DRC including DfID, MONUSCO and the EU.

CONGO'S VIOLENT PEACE

CONFLICT AND STRUGGLE
SINCE THE GREAT AFRICAN WAR

KRIS BERWOUTS

ZED

Zed Books

LONDON

In association with
International African Institute
Royal African Society
World Peace Foundation

Congo's Violent Peace: Conflict and Struggle Since the Great African War
was first published in 2017 by Zed Books Ltd, The Foundry, 17 Oval Way,
London SE11 5RR, UK.

www.zedbooks.net

Typeset in Haarlemmer by seagulls.net
Index by John Harrier
Cover design by Jonathan Pelham
Cover photo © Brian Sokol/UNHCR/Panos

A catalogue record for this book is available from the British Library.

ISBN 978-1-78360-370-1 hb
ISBN 978-1-78360-369-5 pb
ISBN 978-1-78360-371-8 pdf
ISBN 978-1-78360-372-5 epub
ISBN 978-1-78360-373-2 mobi

Printed and bound by CPI Group (UK) Ltd, Croydon, CR0 4YY

With love and respect for Zaida Catalan, Michael J. Sharp,
Pascal Kabungulu, Floribert Chebeya, Serge Maheshe
and all other friends and colleagues who died in their
search for truth and justice for the people of Congo.

'*Three things cannot be long hidden:*
the sun, the moon, and the truth.'
Zaida Catalan quoting Buddha
in her last tweet before she was killed on 12 March 2017.

CONTENTS

ACKNOWLEDGEMENTS

I am very grateful that Zed Books accepted my proposal. Without the support and encouragement of Stephanie Kitchen and Ken Barlow, this book would never have existed. The author's field research was made possible by a working grant of the Pascal Decroos Fund for Investigative Journalism.

It has been fed by the hours of conversation, brainstorming and interviews I had with different people in all corners of the Congolese political and military landscape, opinion makers and civil society activists. The confidential talks I had with them gave me insights about public and hidden agendas on Congo's political scene, formal and less formal attempts to manage the conflicts and find satisfying deals to bring people, parties, communities closer together. I kept my notes and memories since I started to work full time on Central Africa in September 2000. Through this book, I try to share their analysis with the reader.

I want to express my deep gratitude to many Congolese and Congolized friends who gave me access to the common people at grassroot level, the men in the city, the women in the markets and on the fields, people who allowed me to discover Congo from within and who were not afraid to share their hopes and fears with me. I am forever indebted to my friends Chrispin Mvano, Pascal Rukengwa, Jean-Bosco Bahala, Ivan Godfroid, Adolphine Muley, Espérance Twizere, Lambert Mimpiya, Anne-Marie Mukwayanzo, the late Floribert Chebeya, Fergus Thomas, Serge Sivya, Claudia Chuma, Pieter Van Holder, Nestor Bazeye, Maître Célestin Beya, Rosalie Kalanga, Gérard Bisambu, Marie-Noel Cikuru, Eric Kajemba,

Jean-Louis Nzweve, Erik Kennes, Baudouin Hamuli, Patient Bagenda, Kizito Mushizi, Mangaza Walassa, Micheline Mwendike, Jean-Mobert Nsenga, Loochi Muzaliwa, Noel Mayamba, Patrick Ndamubuya, Raph Wakenge, Dieudonné Mirimo, Ornella Kobo, Sylvie Furaha Mwarabu, Manya Riche, Soraya Aziz, Félicien Malanda, Rigobert Minani, Alexis Bouvy and Robert Wangachumo.

Two other friends should also be mentioned: Magnus Taylor, my erstwhile editor at African Arguments, a website hosted by the Royal Africa Society. Magnus ceaselessly stimulated me to publish my analyses and reports of current Congolese affairs. He has spent many hours in putting my drafts into readable and correct English. David Van Reybrouck is also part of this book. We met for the first time in the rather dramatic circumstances he described in *Congo: the epic history of a people* and he has been a *compagnon de route* ever since.

Three friends worked on the manuscript before I submitted it. The Flemish-American poetess Annmarie Sauer corrected my worst crimes against the English language, the young researcher Jonathan Simba Kai helped watch over the coherence of my text, and Gillian Mathys helped me to understand historical dimensions of the land and identity issues I was not even aware of.

Many thanks to all of them.

And most of all to my beloved wife Katelijne. Without her love, patience and understanding, I would not have been able to write this book.

ACRONYMS

AbaKo	Association des BaKongo
ACO	Avenir du Congo
ADF-Nalu	Alliance of Democratic Forces/National Army for the Liberation of Uganda
AFDC	Alliance des Forces Démocratiques du Congo
AFDL	Alliance des forces démocratiques pour la libération du Congo
ALIR	Armée pour la Libération du Rwanda
AMP	Alliance de la Majorité Présidentielle
ANR	Agence Nationale de Renseignements
ARC	Alliance pour le Renouveau du Congo
BCC	Banque Centrale du Congo
CEI	Commission Electorale Indépendante
CENCO	Conférence Episcopale Nationale du Congo
CENI	Commission Electorale Nationale Indépendante
CIAT	Comité International d'Accompagnement de la Transition
CNDD-FDD	Conseil National Pour la Défense de la Démocratie – Forces pour la Défense de la Démocratie
CNDP	Congrès National pour la Défense du Peuple
CNS	Conférence Nationale Souveraine
DDRRR	Disarmament, Demobilization, Repatriation, Reintegration and Resettlement
DRC	Democratic Republic of Congo
EAC	East African Community
EUFOR	European Union Force

EurAc	Réseau Européen pour l'Afrique Centrale
EUSEC	European Mission in support of the Security Sector Reforms in Congo
FARDC	Forces Armées de la République Démocratique du Congo
FAZ	Forces Armées du Zaïre
FDLR	Forces Démocratiques de Libération du Rwanda
FIB	Force Intervention Brigade
FNL	Forces Nationales de Libération
FRF	Forces Républicaines Fédéralistes
G7	Group of seven political parties within the presidential majority who spoke out against a third mandate for Kabila beyond 2016
GDP	Green Democratic Party
GoE	(UN) Group of Experts
HRW	Human Rights Watch
ICC	International Criminal Court
ICHEC	Management school in Brussels
IDPs	Internally displaced persons
IMF	International Monetary Fund
IRC	International Rescue Committee
ICRGL	International Conference on the Great Lakes Region
JMAC	Joint Mission Analysis Center
LRA	Lord's Resistance Army
M23	Mouvement du 23 Mars
MLC	Mouvement de Libération du Congo
MNC	Mouvement National Congolais, Patrice Lumumba's party
MONUC	United Nations Organization Mission in the Democratic Republic of the Congo
MONUSCO	United Nations Organization Stabilization Mission in the Democratic Republic of the Congo
MPR	Mouvement Populaire de la Révolution
MSR	Mouvement Social pour le Renouveau

PALU	Parti Lumumbiste Unifié
PDC	Parti Démocrate Chrétien
PPPD	Parti du Peuple pour la Paix et la Démocratie
PPRD	Parti du Peuple pour la Reconstruction et la Démocratie
PRP	People's Revolutionary Party
PSCF	Peace, Security and Cooperation Framework Agreement
PSI	Social Party Imberakuri
RCD	Rassemblement Congolais pour la Démocratie
RDC	République Démocratique du Congo
RPF	Rwandan Patriotic Front
RTNC	Radio et Télévision Nationale Congolaise
SADC	Southern African Development Community
SSR	Security Sector Reform
UDF-Inkingi	Unified Democratic Forces
UDPS	Union pour la Démocratie et le Progrès Social
UNADEF	Union Nationale des Démocrates et Fédéralistes
UNAFEC	Union des Nationalistes Fédéralistes du Congo
UNC	Union pour la Nation Congolaise
UPC	Union des Patriotes Congolais
VSV	La Voix des Sans-Voix

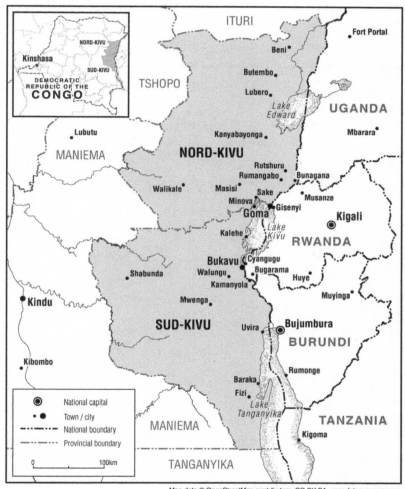

Map data © OpenStreetMap contributors, CC-BY-SA, opendatacommons.org

INTRODUCTION

I know exactly where and when I decided to write this book. In Bukavu, on 21 November 2012. Around teatime. The day before, Goma had fallen into the hands of *Mouvement du 23 Mars* (M23), a rebel group in eastern Congo which had taken up arms against the government in Kinshasa six months earlier. What started as a very localized source of violence brought Congo to the edge of a new implosion, when M23 conquered Goma, the capital of North Kivu, on Tuesday 20 November.

My aim was to take a boat to Goma and then travel further on by plane to Kinshasa. In the hours after Goma's fall, rumours started to whirr in Bukavu too. Someone had been informed of a secret M23 conclave. They would march to Bukavu the next week. Someone else had heard about that conclave too, but he was told (by the friend of a friend) that they would take Bukavu next month. Children came home, trembling. Classmates sent them text messages: M23 had already left Goma, they will be here in the morning. If you dare to go to school after breakfast tomorrow, you will be dead by lunchtime. The trauma of 2004 still hung over this city. In June of that year, Bukavu had been occupied by General Laurent Nkunda's CNDP (*Congrès National pour la Défense du Peuple*), which for ten days had kept the city in an iron grip of looting and rape. The frustration and the anger of the Congolese, their fear for what would come and the feeling of humiliation caused by Goma's fall were tangible ingredients of an explosive cocktail.

The demonstration the next morning spiralled out of control and riots started on the big avenues between the city centre, the harbour and on the way to the airport. The fighting and the burning tyres later spread to the neighbourhoods. Around teatime, everybody went home and the city became quiet again. I left town the next day.

In the meantime I had decided to write this book. Once again Congo was about to collapse, and the best we could hope for was another unworkable 'negotiated solution'. This would euphemistically be categorized as a 'peace agreement', which would lead to a ceasefire and another form of power sharing. But neither the peace agreement, nor the ceasefire, nor the power sharing would contain elements that could lead to sustainable stability or a political structure capable of building confidence and a common agenda between the groups, parties and communities involved. In fact, the fall of Goma revealed the bankruptcy of a misconducted, ill-conceived peace process, very heavily steered by the international community which imposed on Congo a standard package of post-conflict measures, not taking into account the fact that the conflict was never really over. Savage wars and unworkable peace agreements were the result.

The day after Goma's fall I decided to undertake a comprehensive analysis of the conflicts in Congo. This would only be possible if I took the complexity of the conflicts as a starting point, tried to unravel the different layers of conflict and pointed out the importance of conflict at every level. I wanted to analyse how the different peace agreements and international attempts to support them failed to create the conditions for sustainable conflict resolution. They did not significantly strengthen the Congolese state, nor were they able to transform Rwanda's destructive impact on security in eastern Congo into a more constructive cohabitation.

About the time I sent a proposal to Zed, things had changed. M23 had been chased out of the country, and people believed the victory against M23 and the Peace, Security and Cooperation Agreement which had contributed to it could be a turning point towards more stability in the Kivu provinces. But before the contract was signed, the window of opportunity was already shattered. Eventually most of the book was written in a climate of rising tensions related to the approaching 2016 elections. The regime's attempts to push Kabila's regime beyond its constitutional limits created a lot of tensions in the major towns, while in the east local conflicts polarized again. The book was finalized during the last months of 2016 in a repressive political climate when dozens of people had been killed in riots sparked by the fact that the electoral commission had not announced the new elections.

The aim of this book is to identify the different root causes and layers of conflict and the interaction between them, and analyse how they shed light on violence in the Congo, from recent decades until today. The ambition is also to achieve a better understanding of how international interventions, though very expensive, did not create the conditions for the Congolese state to rise from its ashes. We look into the details of the turbulent period of M23, which brought Congo close to a new implosion. Finally, we will see how the momentum after the defeat of M23 faded away and how the lack of progress in the management of the conflict's root causes led to a new crisis and the risk of a new cycle of violence related to the end of Kabila's second and constitutionally last mandate as elected president at the end of 2016.

The conflicts in Congo are too often presented as senseless and perpetual savagery, and with this book I hope to contribute to a more subtle approach with a bottom-up perspective.

Layers of conflict

Central Africa has been shaped by complex regional dynamics, through which local disputes and national conflicts have spilled over borders. Each country in the region has a complex internal situation and a violent recent history, where local antagonisms have become polarized and entangled with those of neighbouring countries. Political, economic and social instability have led to the almost complete dismantling of the state, the political institutions, the justice system, and all administrative structures. The socioeconomic infrastructure has been severely weakened and in Congo's case totally destroyed.

Following the end of the Cold War and throughout the 1990s these regional dynamics have developed into an tsunami of killing and destruction. During the two wars in the Democratic Republic of Congo (DRC), in 1996–1997 and 1998–2002, following the genocide in Rwanda, Congo – and particularly its eastern provinces – became the battlefield of 'Africa's First World War'.[1] The DRC's wealth of natural resources has been an important factor in fuelling conflict as warring factions compete for control of the illegal flow of resources from the DRC into international markets. The result has been a collapsed state, a crisis of impunity and, most of all, a suffering population. Many millions of people[2] have died as a direct or indirect consequence of the fighting, making this the bloodiest conflict since the Second World War. Neither the complex peace process nor the organization of multiparty elections in 2006 and 2011 have been successful in restoring a well-functioning state or in bringing peace and security to the east of Congo.

As a result of the above, people often ask me what the central issue is in the conflict in Central Africa. What are they fighting about? The question is extremely hard to answer. There is no single conflict in eastern Congo. There are at least three layers of recent conflict that come together in a context which is already very complicated because of the difficult cohabitation of different communities and high demographic pressure in an environment where land management is particularly complex. The three layers lifted the conflicts beyond their local impact, overlapping and mutually reinforcing each other: the difficulties of rehabilitating the Congolese state after its various implosions, the continuation of the Rwandan conflict on Congolese territory and the race to exploit the country's abundant mineral resources.

Firstly, there is the struggle for power in Kinshasa after the dismantling of the Congolese state. Within weeks following independence, Congo fell into a constitutional and institutional crisis the country was not able to cope with. The new nation immediately became a pawn on the chessboard of the Cold War. It took years before the government gained control over the entire territory and once that was done, the state was managed with such a degree of bad governance that we had to invent the word 'kleptocracy' for it. State institutions and public mandates were – and to a large extent still are – considered as tools for personal enrichment. The result was a crisis of legitimacy, a ruined state that needed to be rescued from near non-existence, with a total absence of the necessary instruments to guarantee the rule of law. The peace process and the elections of 2006 had created the framework for the Third Republic but they didn't raise the Congolese state from its ashes. It not only remained weak, it also kept its fundamentally predatory nature.[3] A Congolese state with reasonably good governance continues to be a condition for sustainable peace in the region.

Secondly, for many observers, in Congo as well as abroad, the Rwandan government has been responsible for many of the calamities that have beset Congo since the mid-1990s. The Rwandan civil war was exported to Congo in the aftermath of the genocide when two million people fled the Tutsi rebels of the Rwandan Patriotic Front (RPF) on the eve of their victory, while many of these refugees were civilians, this mass of people also contained the remnants of the militias and the defeated army which had initiated the genocide, as well as representatives of the previous government. They were able to organize public life in the camps pretty much according to the schemes and logics of the old regime. The fact that the failure of Mobutu's empire as well as his health had reached a point of no return certainly helped them. Also the massive amount of humanitarian aid injected into the camps allowed the authorities of the defeated regime to build up and reinforce their role in the camps, and to use them as the basis for hit-and-run actions against the new rulers in Kigali.[4] The RPF's reaction to this destabilization eventually accelerated Mobutu's fall and was the first phase in a long process of direct involvement of the Rwandan national army on

Congolese territory. Rwanda's direct interventions did not end the permanent presence of the Rwandan armed opposition which has been responsible for much of the suffering of the citizens of eastern Congo. The Rwandan interventions went along with support for different generations of rebellions put in place by Congolese Tutsi in Kivu. The most recent armed group on this list is M23, which started an uprising against the Congolese state in early 2012. They brought the country close to another implosion by taking the town of Goma in November of the same year and were militarily defeated exactly one year later. The consequences of the Rwandan war and genocide is a major theme of Congo's contemporary history and for many people the ultimate cause of conflict and suffering in Kivu.

Thirdly, an even bigger group of Congolese and foreign Congo-watchers considers the illegal exploitation of mineral resources as the main source of violence in the Congo. Many scholars not only presented the trade in Congo's natural riches as the primary motivation for neighbouring countries to be involved in Congo, but also as the ultimate reason for the long list of foreign or local militias, rebellions and other armed groups competing for control over the different parts of Kivu. Séverine Autesserre describes lucidly how this narrative became dominant, and how it steered the international reaction to the crises in Congo and in the Great Lakes region.[5] UN expert groups, academics, think tanks and specialized NGOs have documented the plundering of Congo's resources since the mid-1990s and produced detailed reports, naming and shaming the political, military and economic actors involved in it. Countries and multilateral institutions as diverse as Germany, the European Union, the OECD, the US, the UN and the World Bank have all elaborated laws and programmes for more controls on mining to prevent the trade in conflict minerals from the DRC.[6] Of course, the 1990s did not create the illegal exploitation of natural resources but changed its direction: Kampala and Kigali became the main axes for minerals leaving Congo and sold on the world market, often passing through East African harbours, the Arab countries or the Indian subcontinent. The scramble for the natural resources of Congo is also a major leitmotiv in the country's and the region's history. King Leopold transformed the Congo into his own Free State, to keep it out of the reach of Belgian public opinion and constitutional instruments which could control the monarch's exploitation. Also under Mobutu, the exploitation and commercialization of then Zaire's natural resources escaped the control of the state because they were organized through parallel and illegal networks to maximize the president's personal enrichment and serve the patronage networks his reign was based on.

The dismantling of the Congolese state, the extension of the Rwandan conflict in Kivu and the illicit exploitation of Congo's natural resources are the most prominent causes of the violence and suffering in eastern Congo. The historical background to these three layers will be explored in Chapter 1. These layers come on top of a complex local environment, with complicated land and identity issues, which will be turned to in Chapter 2.

Chapter 1

THE RESEMBLANCE OF A STATE IN A STATE OF RUIN

Mobutu's legacy

It is impossible to understand how overwhelming the weakness of the Congolese state has been in recent times without having a closer look at its degeneration over the last fifty or so years. Congo experienced its first implosion less than two weeks after independence, on 30 June 1960. The process of decolonization had been poorly prepared and precipitously implemented. The Belgian colonial model was particularly infantalizing: many Congolese only had access to primary school education and a small group were trained to roughly the level of lower civil servants. The country became independent with no more than a handful of university graduates and absolutely no political tradition apart from the attempt to involve the Congolese population in politics at the local level through communal elections in December 1957. Throughout the entire colonial period, the Congolese had been kept out of the more profitable economic sectors and had no access to credit.[1] Thus, there was no managerial capacity whatsoever to take control over the economy.

The power and the state had been handed over to an emerging political landscape crystallizing around a basic cleavage. On the left, there was a group of radicalized nationalists, influenced by the movement of non-aligned countries which started to take shape after the Bandung Conference in 1955 inspired by Kwame Nkrumah's

Pan-African ideology. They considered independence as a first step to a totally new social order, offering better chances to the masses. Prime Minister Patrice Lumumba spearheaded this group. In 1958 he had founded his *Mouvement National Congolais* (MNC), which became the only truly national party able to mobilize people beyond ethnic and regional borders. On the right were leaders considered by the Belgians as much more moderate, less critical about the existing order and interested first and foremost in replacing the top echelons of the colonial pyramid as Congolese *évolués*.[2] Their organizations, often based on region or ethnicity, transformed themselves in the late 1950s into political parties, of which Joseph Kasa-Vubu's Abako (*Association des BaKongo*) was the best organized and the most powerful.[3] For this group, Congo's future should be federal, with strong provinces. The financial and economic lobbies in Europe and in North America obviously were in favour of Kasa-Vubu's vision, and the Eisenhower administration in Washington was afraid that Lumumba could become an African counterpart of Fidel Castro, who had recently come to power in Cuba.[4]

A mutiny broke out on 4 July when the Belgian commander-in-chief of the new Congolese army wrote on a blackboard 'Before independence = after independence' and on 11 July the governor of Katanga, Moïse Tshombe, declared the prosperous mining province independent. The Belgian government immediately sent advisors and 8,000 paratroopers to protect the rebellious province against the Congolese national army. The United Nations adopted a resolution to support Lumumba's government in restoring order and national integrity. The first blue helmets arrived on 18 July. Congo's first war had started in the very first month of independence. A few weeks later, the diamond-mining province of South Kasai quit Congo as well.[5]

The national chaos inevitably plunged the government into a deep crisis. President Kasa-Vubu dismissed Prime Minister Lumumba on 5 September, and one week later he dissolved the Parliament. On 14 September the young army chief of staff, Joseph-Désiré Mobutu, neutralized the government, left Kasa-Vubu in office but put Lumumba under house arrest. In January 1961 Mobutu delivered Lumumba to his arch-enemies, the secessionist regime of Katanga. He was killed on the 17th.[6]

What followed was a period of nearly five years of successive unstable governments which never succeeded in getting the entire country under control. The secessionist wars came to an end but in early 1964 a new uprising started, led by Lumumba's former minister of education, Pierre Mulele, who managed to gain control of more than half of the country in a few months.[7] On 24 November 1965 Mobutu neutralized the government for the second time. This time he had come to stay: he took full control over the state apparatus. He deposed Kasa-Vubu and became president himself.

Congo went through thirty-two years of neo-colonial dictatorship under Mobutu, supported by Europe and the United States to safeguard Western economic interests in the mining sector and as a bastion against communism in Africa on the geo-strategic chessboard of the Cold War. Mobutu took and consolidated power in a period when a number of African heads of state declared themselves adepts of African or Arab socialism. Between 1965 and 1969, leaders such as Kwameh Nkrumah (Ghana), Julius Nyerere (Tanzania), Kenneth Kaunda (Zambia), Milton Obote (Uganda), Muammar el-Ghaddafi (Libya) and Gaafar Nimeiry (Sudan) wanted to transform society based on authentic African values such as solidarity and communal life, which they considered as having common roots with socialism. Mobutu received Western support because he was perceived as being able to block the rise of the socialist regimes on the continent.

The early years of Mobutu's presidency brought optimism after years of chaos. His rule enjoyed broad support, the country stabilized and a relatively effective administration was installed. Mobutu 'pacified' Congo (at least he killed Mulele and defeated his insurrection) in 1968 and started to demilitarize his regime. He began to wear civilian clothes for public appearances and introduced the accessories of traditional chiefdom like the leopard-skin hat and the carved ebony walking stick.[8] The main instrument to exercise his rule became the political party he had founded in 1967, the MPR (*Mouvement Populaire de la Révolution*), which soon became the only party allowed in Congo. Mobutu did not invent the single-party state but he refined the concept of a ruling party by proclaiming that every citizen was a party member by birth. '*Olinga olinga te, ozali na kati ya MPR*', the people sighed. 'Whether you want it or not, you are in the MPR.'[9]

The MPR became the engine of the patrimonial system Mobutu set up to manage the extensive patronage networks which covered all areas of public life, and corruption was the fuel to keep it running. But in the mid-1970s the machinery started to sputter because copper prices collapsed and oil prices were skyrocketing. Meanwhile, the burden of indebtedness rose dramatically because of the white elephant prestige projects built by foreign companies and equipped with the most sophisticated materials and technology. They were conceived as beacons for Zaire's triumphant entry into modernity but in practice turned out to be total disasters because the economic output never came close to expectations. The Inga–Shaba power line, the Makulu steel mill and the Tenge-Fugurume copper mines are iconic examples of colossal investments without return.

Mobutu ruled over Congo in full respect of King Leopold's tradition, exploiting the country as if it were his personal property.[10] In 1971, he tried to give his regime its own ideological content through *zaïrisation*, an authenticity campaign which was meant to be a kind of cultural upgrading of African pre-colonial identity as an attractive alternative to African socialism. The country, many cities and even the citizens were given new names, supposedly rooted in local history. But its main – very negative – impact was economic: the expropriation of European-owned industries and other enterprises in the medium term was economic suicide for Mobutism, because the means of production were divided among the elite of the regime, often people without the vision, competence or will to manage in a responsible or sustainable way what had been entrusted to them. By 1974, greed and incompetence had destroyed most of Zaire's economy.[11]

When Mobutu's state ceased to have the cash to service the clientelistic networks it had created, it lost its remaining legitimacy.[12] Jan Vansina concluded in 1982:

> Legitimacy is gone, citizens are alienated. Naked power and bribes erode the law. In turn the strongly centralized state has lost much of its effective grip, because its legal directives are ignored, except under duress or when they seem to be opportune.[13]

This lack of legitimacy could only be compensated by the dividends drawn from his status as the most reliable ally of the West on the continent. All sectors of the state machinery crumbled. The process was fastest and most visible in the army:

> Soldiers took military vehicles away from the base and used them to run their own taxi services. Radios and record players disappeared from the mess halls, bulldozers and trucks from the garages. Officers even took their subordinates home with them and used them as servants.[14]

Very soon mismanagement had assumed such endemic proportions that Congo-watchers started to define the process as self-cannibalization of the Congolese state.[15] The second half of Mobutu's reign has been presented by scholars as a classic example of state failure, with its often deadly cocktail of violence, dictatorship and corruption resulting in the complete failure of the economy and the total destruction of the state.

Mobutu was very much a product of the Cold War and his days were numbered when it finally came to an end. As with many of his fellow presidents in Africa, he had felt for decades that he had carte blanche from the West regarding the internal politics of his country. Now, though, all of a sudden democracy and human rights mattered in Africa too.

A wave of optimism was palpable in international politics. At last the arms race would end and enormous amounts of money which had previously been used for building up military power could now be invested in sustainable development and the struggle against poverty. Intellectuals predicted the end of ideology and history, and very soon even the end of nation states. But that did not happen. The initial euphoria was rapidly halted by the emergence of violent nationalism in Yugoslavia, the rise of ultra-orthodox Islam in the Muslim world and of extreme-right parties in Europe. It was in Africa that the proclaimed new world order made way for a new chaos. Civil wars resulted in the implosion of states in countries such as Liberia, Sierra Leone, Somalia and those of Central Africa. The accelerated democratization processes, imposed due to the end of the Cold War, created conflicts which were different from those that had existed earlier, with widespread outbursts of extreme violence characterized by shocking numbers of civilians among the victims as well as among the perpetrators of violence. It caused not only massive waves of displaced people and refugees, but also the complete destruction of the state and its instruments, leaving the population in total disarray due to the disintegration of social and institutional networks. The living conditions of a huge part of the population dropped to a previously unseen level. The international community lacked both operational power and political will to stop massive crimes against humanity, humanitarian disasters and genocides.[16]

The 'Great African War'

In the early morning of 7 April 1994 all hell broke loose in Rwanda. A few hours earlier, President Juvénal Habyarimana's plane had been shot down and crashed in the garden of his own palace. He was returning from Tanzania, where he had been attending a regional summit about the implementation of the peace agreement between the regime, based on the Hutu majority, and the Tutsi rebels of the RPF, who had grown up in Rwandan refugee camps in Uganda and had started an armed struggle in October 1990. Habyarimana's death triggered an unprecedented massacre of between 700,000 and a million Tutsis and moderate Hutus, the genocide only ending with the military victory of the RPF in July 1994, as a result of which two million Hutus fled to Congo. Rwanda stabilized but violence continued in Congo and eventually led to what was later called the Great African War, fought on Congolese soil by soldiers from the regular armies of nine other African countries and numerous foreign and local armed groups.

As the RPF was about to win the war against the remnants of the late Habyarimana's government and thus put an end to the genocide, there was a massive exodus of Hutu refugees to Rwanda's neighbours. The vast majority of them, about two million, ended up in huge refugee camps in the Zairian provinces of North and South Kivu. Almost immediately, the regular army and the militias involved in the genocide reorganized life along the old lines, forcing the people to live under their authority and continuing the war by other means.[17] The disintegration of the Zairian state and the illness of its dictator Mobutu gave what was left of the fleeing Rwandan army greater scope to operate without disturbance.

Very soon the camps became an excellent base for hit-and-run actions intent on destabilizing the new leaders in Kigali. In order to put an end to these infiltrations, Rwanda invaded its giant neighbour twice with the support of Uganda. The first time (1996–1997) led to a change of regime in Kinshasa. The war started in October 1996, when the Rwandan and Ugandan armies used the deterioration of the relationship between Zairian Kinyarwanda-speaking communities (in the first place the Banyamulenge – Tutsi from South Kivu) and the other communities as a pretext to invade Zaire and attack the refugee camps. Uvira fell on 28 October, followed by Bukavu two days later. The aim was to dismantle the camps and neutralize the armed forces of Habyarimana's regime in order to stop their military actions against the new leaders. Gérard Prunier estimated in 2009 that the death toll among the refugees was around 300,000.[18]

In 2010, the United Nations published the Democratic Republic of the Congo 1993–2003 UN Mapping Report. In response to the discovery of three mass graves in eastern Congo in late 2005, the UN mandated an Expert Panel to conduct a mapping exercise of the most serious violations of human rights and international humanitarian law committed within the territory of the DRC between March 1993 and June 2003. The 550-page report contains descriptions of 617 alleged violent incidents, backed up by at least two independent sources. The report covers in detail how the Hutu refugee camps were dismantled in October 1996, how hundreds of thousands of Hutu refugees fled deeper into Congo's vast hinterland, and how they were pursued and massacred by the Rwandan and Ugandan armies and their Congolese ally, *Alliance des Forces Démocratiques pour la Libération du Congo* (AFDL). The mapping report team noted that 'The question of whether the numerous serious acts of violence committed against the Hutus (refugees and others) constitute crimes of genocide has attracted a significant degree of comment and to date remains unresolved'. The report repeatedly stresses that this question can 'only be decided by a court decision on the basis of evidence beyond all reasonable doubt'. However, 'the apparent systematic and widespread attacks described in this report reveal a number of inculpatory elements that, if proven before a competent court, could be characterized as crimes of genocide'.[19]

To give their campaign a local façade, the Rwandans and Ugandans had handpicked a Zairean rebel, Laurent-Désiré Kabila, as one of the leaders of a new coalition against Mobutu, the AFDL. At independence, Kabila, born in 1939, was a young politician from northern Katanga's Luba-speaking community (the Balubakat) who had supported Lumumba's regime. He made a tour through Eastern Europe after Lumumba's death, joined the radical insurrection of Pierre Mulele and became his minister of foreign affairs. When Che Guevara visited Kivu in 1965, he saw in Kabila one of the few leaders with the revolutionary potential of a mass leader, even if he was afraid that Kabila's lack of revolutionary seriousness and his penchant for booze and women would probably stand between Kabila and his victory.[20] In 1967, Kabila and the remnants of his supporters moved to the south of South Kivu and founded the People's Revolutionary Party (PRP). Kabila was the only rebel leader of his generation who was never defeated or bought off by Mobutu, and he was able to maintain the mountainous area around Fizi and Baraka as a mini-enclave. From the late 1970s, his interests seemed to shift away from his struggle and he acquired considerable wealth through gold and timber trade on Lake Tanganyika and real estate in Tanzania. Kabila and his PRP soon overshadowed the other three parties and leaders within the new rebellion.[21]

It took the rebels and their allies seven months to chase Mobutu out of Zaire. In most places, the AFDL could progress without much resistance from Mobutu's army, the FAZ (Forces Armées du Zaïre). Prunier estimated their number to be 'at the most fifty thousand, with probably less than half at anything like fighting capacity',[22] unmotivated, unpaid, abandoned to themselves. On 25 December, Bunia was taken. The capital of Ituri was one of the few places where serious fighting occurred. Kindu followed on 28 February. An important symbolic turning point was the taking of Kisangani on 15 March.[23] The city was in the bend of the mighty Congo river, the country's artery, and as such an open way to the undefended capital. Mobutu, terminally ill, left Zaire and on 17 May 1997 the AFDL soldiers walked into Kinshasa. Kabila arrived in town on 20 May and took the oath as president of the country on 29 May. Zaire became the Democratic Republic of Congo again; and on 7 September the man who had sworn that he would never be referred to as 'the ex-president of Zaire' died in exile in Morocco.

Of course, this victory would never have been achieved without the Rwandan and Ugandan armies taking the lead and the benevolent support of part of the Western world, in the first place the United States and the United Kingdom. These countries felt profoundly guilty for the international community's passivity in the face of the Rwandan genocide. Because of this guilt, the Rwandan regime could count on empathy and support. Furthermore, personalities like Uganda's Yoweri Museveni and Rwanda's Paul Kagame were believed to represent a more positive generation of African leaders who could guide the continent into a new era and help it forget iconic predecessors like Mobutu, Idi Amin or Bokassa.[24] They hoped that Kabila would become one of them although not everybody saw him as a role model of forward-looking leadership. Prunier called Kabila

> a political Rip van Winkle whose conspiratorial political style had been frozen at some point back in the 1960s and who still lived in a world seen strategically as a deadly struggle against imperialism and tactically as a mixture of conspiracies and informal economics.[25]

His government was a medley of people with different backgrounds, half of them from the diaspora, some technocrats and some ideologues, some labelled as progressive and others as conservative, some experienced and others new, but all of them overshadowed by the overwhelming personality of *Mzee*,[26] who 'seemed to think that pitting these various men (and groups they represented) against each other would enable him to remain in full control of what one hesitates to call the "state apparatus"'.[27]

Despite efforts to pay the soldiers, Kabila did not manage to transform the *kadogos* (young soldiers without experience who conquered the country for him, many of them minors) of his rebel army into an effective national army. Internationally, meanwhile, he lost credit because of the smokescreen he maintained around the question of the hundreds of thousands of 'disappeared' Hutu refugees during the seven months of the war.

His regime basically relied on Rwanda after the military victory. Rwandan officials occupied strategic positions in the government. Despite James Kaberebe's position as the acting chief of staff of the army, Kivu remained the operational base from where the armed opposition against Kagame continued its incursions into Rwanda. Relations with the Rwandans quickly deteriorated, not helped by negative Congolese public opinion, which saw that Rwanda's role had not been downscaled after Mobutu's defeat and started to see Kabila as the marionette of his ally. On 27 July 1998, Kabila published a communiqué ordering all Rwandan and Ugandan troops to leave the country. On 29 July, 600 Rwandan soldiers fled from Kinshasa back to Kigali.[28]

The second war started on 2 August 1998. Fifteen months after taking over the country, Kabila's former allies Rwanda and Uganda started a new military campaign with the aim of chasing Kabila out of the country and replacing him as soon as possible. Goma, Bukavu and Uvira fell in the first few days of the war. Two weeks after the start of the war, it was claimed that these cities had been taken by a new Congolese rebel movement, RCD (*Rassemblement Congolais pour la Démocratie*), a hodgepodge of ex-Mobutists, discontented AFDL members, opposition leaders who had been imprisoned and tortured by Kabila's services, people with a civil society background and some leading intellectuals such as former UNESCO staff member Z'Ahidi Ngoma and Professor Ernest Wamba dia Wamba.[29] But it was obvious from the beginning that the military progress of this rebellion was welcomed by Rwandan and Ugandan troops under the command of the Rwandan army chief of staff James Kaberebe. And it was clear that Kabila's army was no match for them.

As the front in Kivu developed well for Rwanda, it was decided to open a second front in the west. Kaberebe commandeered 180 Rwandan, Ugandan and Congolese soldiers with weapons and ammunition in a Boeing 707 at Goma airport and flew them 1,500 km to the military airbase of Kitona, at the mouth of the Congo river, 250 km west of Kinshasa. They took the garrison by surprise and captured the town. This masterstroke brought Kinshasa within reach. More soldiers were flown in from the east and by 13 August not only Boma and Matadi had been captured, but also the Inga dam, the huge hydroelectric power plant on the Congo river. Kabila and most of his ministers left the capital for Lubumbashi. When the rebels cut the power supply, the fall of the city seemed imminent.[30]

Kabila was saved by the Southern African Development Community (SADC) countries: on 19 August, 400 Zimbabwean soldiers entered Congo and four days later the Angolan army started reconquering the Bas-Congo province. Kabila had brought Congo into the SADC and the support he got from its member states was decisive. If Congo had tried to stand alone, as it had two years earlier, it would have collapsed in less than a month.

A third SADC member, Namibia, stepped in as well. In the north of the continent further allies were found. Sudan decided to support Congo because of the former's ongoing conflict with Uganda, which supported rebels in South Sudan. Libya's President Ghaddafi contributed a few airplanes in an attempt to reduce his international isolation, and Chad sent 2,000 soldiers as a gesture of solidarity with Sudan and Libya.[31] On the other side of the front, the rebels were supported by Rwanda, Uganda and to a lesser extent Burundi.

Rwanda had to withdraw from the western front but the *blitzkrieg* in the east continued: with the support of nine Rwandan and five Ugandan battalions, the RCD managed to capture Kisangani, Watsa and Moba by early September. Kindu, the capital of the Maniema province, fell on 12 October.[32] Strategically, this was an important loss for Kinshasa: Kindu offered not only access to the Kasai and its diamonds; it was also the airport nearest to the Rwandan border.

By mid-November, Uganda had created a new rebel movement around Jean-Pierre Bemba, the *Mouvement de Libération du Congo* (MLC). Jean-Pierre was the son of Saolona Bemba, one of Mobutu's associates who had benefited from the *zaïrisation* campaign in the 1970s and had managed to build an economic empire on it. He graduated from the prestigious Catholic Institute of Higher Commercial Studies (ICHEC in French) in Brussels. His father had been arrested by Kabila for being a collaborator of the *ancien régime*, but was released after paying half a million dollars.[33] By supporting Bemba, Uganda had a proxy rebel group of its own and started to withdraw from the RCD. Very soon, the Uganda-oriented wing of the RCD left the movement and founded its own rebellion, with headquarters in Kisangani, under the name RCD-K. The RCD wing under Rwandan influence was referred to as RCD-Goma because it maintained its base in the capital of North Kivu.

This policy made clear that the alliance between Rwanda and Uganda was not strong and eventually led to several confrontations between the two armies (in May 1999, June 2000 and May 2002), with the city of Kisangani as the battlefield and thousands of Congolese citizens as collateral damage. These confrontations became 'the graveyard of Rwandan and Ugandan reputations'[34] because they made clear that Rwanda and Uganda were not only in Congo out of domestic security concerns, as they had been claiming since the first war started in 1996. Both countries had fought three battles on foreign soil for the control of one of the region's main hubs of the diamond trade.

The RCD was able to control the towns it took, but was never able to impose itself in the rural areas, where there was heavy fighting between the RCD and different armed groups. One of them was the remnant of the Interahamwe and FAZ, Rwandan Hutu who had organized and implemented the genocide. They had reorganized themselves after the Rwandan army had dismantled the refugee camps in October 1996 under the label of ALIR (*Armée pour la Libération du Rwanda*) and had attacked targets in Rwanda. After August 1998, they would confront the Rwandan army on Congolese soil. In September 2000, ALIR merged into a new and broader armed group of Rwandan Hutu, the FDLR (*Forces Démocratiques de Libération du Rwanda*).

The other challenger of the RCD in Kivu was a loose movement of ultra-nationalist Congolese guerrillas using the label Mai Mai. The name refers to the water they used in their rituals which allegedly made them invulnerable to the enemy's bullets. Mai Mai groups had mushroomed spontaneously all over the occupied territories. Their combatants were 'reckless, confused, mostly very young, poorly armed and organized, and often so violent that they were feared by the population they purported to defend'.[35] They fought the RCD and the Rwandan army but were not strong enough to protect the population against their violent revenge. Kabila's regular army had been chased out of Kivu but he relied on the Rwandan armed opposition and the Mai Mai to prevent the RCD from controlling the countryside in eastern Congo.

In early 1999 the front froze along the Ikela–Lodja–Kabinda–Pweto line. The west and the south of Congo was under the control of Kabila and his allies, Rwanda and its ally RCD-Goma controlled much of the east, while Uganda with the MLC and RCD-K controlled much of the northern province of Equateur and bits of Orientale province.

Rape and sexual violence

Events in Congo, especially in the eastern provinces, have resulted in a culture of violence becoming a state of lawlessness and total impunity, where justice has ceased to exist, where militias are organized, disintegrate and escape any form of control, where regular armies become the major source of insecurity and where rape is commonly used as a weapon of war.

This problem of rape in Central Africa does not find its roots in the civil wars into which the region was plunged from the 1990s, although it is obvious that these wars have contributed to the exponential growth of sexual violence. Rather, during my years researching DRC I have seen sexual violence emerge in three phases. In the first phase, rape is a gruesome offshoot of the conflict, part of the right of the victor. A militia entering a conquered town celebrates its victory by plundering the houses, slaughtering the goats, drinking the beer and raping the women. *La chosification de la femme*, as they call it in Congo, the crime of reducing a woman to a thing.

In the second phase, rape becomes a weapon that is deployed in a very systematic way against a community to break it, and to strike it in its most intimate and most vulnerable part: its womb. The physical, psychological and emotional consequences are very heavy to bear for the victim and her family. The social stigma is devastating because many raped women and girls are rejected by their husbands or fathers. Sexual violence creates a climate in which women cannot go to the fields, where girls do not dare go to school. Therefore it destroys the social and economic cohesion of society.

In the third phase, when the conflict seems to be moving towards a solution, rape is the only form of human rights violation that does not diminish, which is extremely worrying. The damage caused by sexual violence does not stop with a peace agreement or a ceasefire. The perpetrators are no longer the warring parties or militias, but the regular security forces and increasingly unarmed actors such as family members, neighbours, friends and teachers. This means that sexual violence penetrates the values and the culture, and that the 'thingification' of woman is a very hard process to reverse. There are no quick solutions to rape.

The peace process

In June 1999, the Zambian president Frederic Chiluba took the initiative to bring the countries involved in the war in Congo and the rebel movements RCD and MLC to the negotiation table with representatives from the United Nations, the African Union (AU) and SADC. On 10 July, an agreement was signed in Lusaka. Signatories were leaders of six countries involved in the conflict: Angola, the DRC, Namibia, Rwanda, Uganda and Zimbabwe. The leaders of the rebel groups did not sign. The parties agreed the cessation of hostilities between all the belligerent forces in the DRC within twenty-four hours after the signing of the agreement. According to the terms of the agreement, forty-five days later the government of the DRC, the armed opposition, namely the RCD and MLC, as well as the unarmed opposition were to enter into an open national dialogue, including with *les forces vives* (the living forces) of civil society, with the help of a neutral international facilitator. Later, former president of Botswana, Ketumile Masire, was appointed to this role. After four months all the foreign armies were to move out of the Congo and be replaced by a UN force. Two months after that, Kinshasa and the rebels were to have integrated their respective armed forces and would sit down to discuss a democratic government of transition.[36]

The implementation of the action plan of the Lusaka Agreement did not progress at all. The timetable was utterly unrealistic and the signatories had not agreed on a supervisory mechanism. Both sides tried to delay the implementation and the lack of diplomatic credibility reduced the conflict again to its bare military dimension. Many actors and observers considered President Kabila, whom they accused of 'deliberately torpedoing the MONUC deployment, of humiliating Masire and of mocking the international community',[37] as particularly counterproductive to a negotiated peace agreement.

On 16 January 2001, President Kabila was shot in his palace by one of his bodyguards, former child soldier Rachidi Kasereka. The assassin tried to escape but was shot on the spot by the presidential aide-de-camp.

Congo has always been a breeding ground for conspiracy theories and many wild scenarios have circulated around Kabila's death. The most likely scenarios can be classified into two categories: he had been killed by his enemies or by his friends. For many, the assassination had been masterminded by Rwanda, making use of his bodyguards by playing on their grudge related to the way Kabila had eliminated his three co-founders of the AFDL in the earliest phase of the first war.[38] But others believe that Kabila died because his allies, in the first place Angola but also Zimbabwe, increasingly considered him the main obstacle to ending a costly war which weighed negatively on public opinion in those countries. They wanted to support the present regime in Kinshasa but observed a head of state increasingly isolated in Congo as well as on the diplomatic front. The prospects for a negotiated solution had become very bleak after the battle of Pweto in December 2000, in which the armies of Congo, Angola and Zimbabwe had suffered a crushing defeat due to poor military leadership, with tremendous loss of men, equipment and munitions. One month later, Kabila was dead.

Laurent-Désiré Kabila was succeeded by his son Joseph, twenty-nine years old, recently appointed general and chief of staff of the land army. He had very little political experience. He was born in his father's liberated zone in the south of South Kivu, but had spent most of his youth in Tanzania and Uganda. He had very little knowledge about Congo's history and geography, and was not fluent in French or Lingala, dominant languages on the scene of national politics in Congo. For these reasons and because of his natural shyness, Joseph Kabila was considered a weak president, almost a marionette, probably a transitional figure.

The succession of Laurent-Désiré by Joseph Kabila was a turning point. In a few months, the young president managed to reshuffle the government and put aside most of those considered as hawks of his father's regime. He met Museveni and Kagame and managed remarkably well to create the feeling within the wider international community that maybe a negotiated solution, along the lines of the Lusaka Agreement his father had blocked so obstinately, would be possible.

Eventually, after a false start or two, the Inter-Congolese Dialogue took off on 26 February 2002 in the surrealistic venue of Sun City, a former luxury holiday resort for Sun City executives. The negotiations lasted for weeks without visible progress, but on 19 April, two days before the end of the talks, an unexpected agreement was reached between the government, Bemba's MLC and most of the opposition parties, civil society representatives and the Mai Mai groups. The RCD-Goma and the UDPS (*Union pour la Démocratie et le Progrès Social*), the historical opposition party with its flamboyant leader Etienne Tshisekedi, who had challenged Mobutu since the end of the 1970s, were the most prominent non-signatories. The agreement was an important achievement, even if it has never been fully implemented. It was a first step towards the reunification of the country – for the first time in many years it was possible to fly from Kinshasa to Mbandaka, Beni or Butembo. Eventually a global and inclusive agreement was signed by all parties on 17 December 2002 in Pretoria. The main result of the agreement was a transition of two years, which could be extended twice by six months, during which the country would be administered by a government of national unity using a complex system of power sharing which was baptized 1 + 4. This construction was fully supported by the international community by increasing the UN Mission in the DRC MONUC's operatives to 8,700 and in the following years gradually to 16,700, and by the installation of CIAT (*Comité international d'accompagnement de la transition*), a structure through which the main bilateral and multilateral partners monitored the process.[39] CIAT was not an advisory body but a formal part of the Agreement of Pretoria and thus an official institution of the transition. In fact, the involvement of the international community was so high-placed and formalized that many observers considered it a guardianship and as such a limitation on Congo's sovereignty.[40]

In the meantime, Rwanda and Uganda had accepted, started and finished the withdrawal of their troops from Congolese territory. Between September and November 2002, 30,000 foreign soldiers left the country, even if there were immediately suspicions that especially Rwanda's withdrawal had not been complete.

With the exit of the foreign troops and an inclusive agreement signed by all Congolese political actors, the two major components of the Lusaka Agreement had been implemented. This did not stop the violence, especially in eastern Congo, but it reduced the fighting from a continental war to a regional low-intensity conflict. The Great African War was over, it seemed. I was regularly in Congo in those days, as programme officer of a Belgian NGO working on human rights and democratization. I immediately felt the difference in Kivu: former frontlines ceased to exist; traffic and commerce were boosted so that, for instance, the price of rice drastically dropped in the cities. The impact was felt within weeks.

A lot had come together in the Great African War: the Mobutu empire arrived at its predictable end, accelerated by the changing world order and the fact that Mobutu was no longer indispensable as a bastion against communism in Africa. The crumbling state had lost its capacity to handle local conflict and the Rwandan genocide overflowed onto Congolese territory, triggering a confrontation between regular armies and militias from many African countries. This created an extremely chaotic situation with many destructive consequences, including what was a violent environment becoming a state of total impunity, and the transformation of a highly informal economy into a war economy through rapid militarization. All this took place with an international community in the background which was unable or unwilling to get involved and lacked knowledge as to the root causes of what was really happening on the ground.

Rich soil, poor people

Calling the Congo a geological scandal has become a standard expression. It refers to many natural resources and many eras. David Van Reybrouck summarizes it from the rubber in early colonial days up to the age of mobile phones:

> It was almost too good to be true. Until then, the economic exploitation of the area had aimed exclusively at its biological riches – ivory and rubber – but now a far greater wealth was found to be lying a few meters under the ground. Katanga, the rather unpromising region that Leopold had annexed almost by accident in 1884, suddenly turned out to contain an improbably vast treasure trove.[41]

Not only copper and uranium were found, but also zinc, cobalt, tin, gold, wolfram, manganese, tantalum and anthracite coal. When the incomes from rubber started to drop, other minerals became profitable:

> It seemed like a historical déjà vu: in the same way the rubber boom had arrived just in time to offset the dwindling ivory trade, mining began just in time to replace the ailing rubber industry ... During the last century and a half, whenever acute demand has arisen on the international market for a given raw material – ivory in the Victorian era; rubber after the invention of the inflatable tire; copper during the full-out industrial and military expansion; uranium during the Second World War and later in the Cold War, alternative electrical energy during the oil crisis of the 1970s; coltan in the age of portable telephonics.[42]

But this history was always a tragic balance between abundance and great misery, because fabulous profits were made but did not trickle down to the larger part of the population.

Mobutu's Zaire had been a geological scandal indeed, but that doesn't mean that it was at the epicentre of the international mining trade, at least by the second half of Mobutu's reign. The sector had been, as with other sectors of public life, in steady decline since the 1980s and in free fall from the early 1990s onwards.[43] The countries involved in overthrowing Mobutu did not do so in the first place out of greed for Congo's minerals, but because the armed opposition against them operated from Zairian soil. Trade became more important as their march on Kinshasa advanced and they managed to deprive the government of its control over much of its territory. That attracted risk-seeking entrepreneurs from all over the world.[44]

But this was different during the second war, when Rwanda and Uganda made a new incursion into Congo, this time to replace their former ally Laurent-Désiré Kabila. From 1998 until the war's official end in 2002, natural resources were no longer side effects of the war but increasingly became the most important motivation and stake of the conflict. This was not only true for the countries supporting the rebels but also for the allies mobilized by the government in Kinshasa. In both cases the plundering of Congo was systematically organized with the help of Congolese elites.

The overlap between military objectives and parallel illegal economic activities started to influence the military decision-making regarding the deployment of troops and defining operational zones. Between April 2000 and October 2002, a Panel of Experts with a mandate from the Security Council produced three reports on the illegal exploitation of natural resources. They worked in the first place on the exploitation of the resources in the eastern part of the country by Rwanda and Uganda (gold, diamonds, cassiterite, coltan and timber) but also on the plundering by Zimbabwe, Angola and Namibia, paying back their support of the Congolese government by helping themselves through mining concessions.

Filip Reyntjens, in his book *The Great African War*, estimates that in 2000 the Rwandan army generated between $50 and $100 million through the exploitation and trade of coltan. The official Rwandan budget for defence in that same year was $86 million. Congo's natural resources not only provided the invisible part of Rwanda's defence budget, they also bought the loyalty of the political, military and economic elite in favour of a Rwandan regime that was never as monolithic or coherent as it wanted to be.[45]

The eastern provinces were formally under the control of the RCD rebels, who were too weak and too few to govern. In practice, control was exercised by the Rwandan army (with more and better trained soldiers) and civil servants. In Rwanda itself, a Congo Desk was created in Kigali to organize the direct exploitation of Congolese natural resources as efficiently as possible.[46] In practice, it was a channel for military and political leaders to commercialize part of the Congolese minerals without passing through the official accounts of the Rwandan state. Rwanda always denied the existence of a Congo Desk as an actual institution, but it grew bigger and eventually became a kind of a state within the state.[47]

Thus Congolese natural resources not only generated the funds to cover the military expenses, they were also the main source of personal enrichment for the Rwandan elite. As the Report of the Expert Panel of October 2002 stated, the activities around the Congo Bureau contributed $320 million to the military expenses of Rwanda, and had a huge impact on Rwanda's foreign affairs policy and other official decisions. The panel estimated that 60% to 70% of the coltan that left from eastern Congo was exported under the direct supervision of Rwandan national army commanders, from small airports in the immediate surroundings of mines to Kigali or Cyangugu.

Several well-informed sources, including the UN Group of Experts (GoE) and highly specialized NGOs such as Global Witness, Raid and Ipis, have pointed out that within the mining areas, Congolese civilians were forced to work without payment, or forced to sell minerals to Rwandan officers at a very 'preferential' rate.

The result was that the informal economy in eastern Congo was militarized to the point that the continuation of the state of lawlessness, with very serious negative impacts on the situation on the ground in terms of security and human rights, became a condition for the continued and systematic plundering of natural resources.

The concrete result was that, at a grassroots level, the execution of power became very violent. Armed forces used intimidation and exploitation, and killed people. In the absence of a properly functioning state, militias and rebel groups exploited mines, controlled trade routes and imposed all manner of taxes on the population, including import and export taxes. Road blocks were set up around markets and on the main roads to rob farmers and other people of their goods or money. There were fixed rates for pedestrians and vehicles. In areas controlled by the RCD-Goma, there were annual taxes on vehicles and a range of taxes on individual trips, road tolls and insurance. Filip Reyntjens calls the process 'the privatization and criminalization of public space' as a result of the state's collapse, carried out by a small core of political and military elites, rebel leaders and businessmen, working together for personal enrichment (only in the case of Rwanda were the profits partly used in an institutional way).[48] The illegal channels ran through Kampala and Kigali, and to a lesser extent through Bujumbura with the active involvement of the respective governments. But of course, in an increasingly globalized economy, governments were only intermediaries in a mass of complex, international and rapidly mutating trading networks. Kagame and Museveni were not at the end of any supply line. It was the multinational mining companies, shady fly-by-nights, notorious but highly evasive arms dealers and crooked businessmen in Switzerland, Russia, Kazakhstan, Belgium, the Netherlands and Germany that made a killing by selling Congo's stolen raw materials. They all operated in an extremely free market-place. In political terms Congo was a disaster area but in economic terms it was a paradise – at least for some. Failed nation states are the success stories of runaway global neoliberalism.[49]

The Great African War was not the root cause of the plundering of Congo's natural resources. Parallel circuits of exploitation had existed since King Leopold's days and were the backbone of Mobutu's Zaïre. But the 1990s changed the course and the destination of these circuits. Because of the systematic and massive plundering of natural resources by Rwanda and Uganda, many observers started to see it as the main cause of war in Congo. I never did, because that would prevent us from analysing the conflicts in their full complexity. Even so, it is a very important dimension, and the reason why the conflicts were self-financing: the parties, militias and other key players never ran dry due to the illicit exploitation of resources.

Chapter 2

IN SEARCH OF ROOT CAUSES

The importance of local conflict: land and identity

We started this book with the dismantling of the state under Mobutu and we saw how its remnants were swept away by two wars which were initiated by the Rwandan post-genocide regime. We saw how at some point during these wars the focus shifted more and more to the illicit exploitation of Congo's abundant natural resources. For some key players on the ground, their economic interests became the most important stake in the fighting. For many armies or armed groups, the war paid itself back through the trade in conflict minerals. The three layers of conflict outlined in the introduction overlap and reinforce each other, but none of them can be reduced to being merely a part of one of the others. They are relatively recent developments coming on top of a complex environment of increasing demographic pressure and competition between communities about access to land.

Before colonization in the nineteenth century, eastern Congo consisted of a large number of small kingdoms, and polities with different degrees of centralization. In other zones, the most important socio-political institution was the clan. These polities did not necessarily coincide with an ethnic map of Kivu in the twenty-first century. The important Shi community of South Kivu, for instance, consisted of several kingdoms with differing degrees of political centralization. Between these proto-states and communities, competition for power and control over economic resources was highly complex and dynamic.

These kingdoms were in a constant process of expansion and contraction. Land was important for communities of farmers and livestock breeders – it represented wealth and prestige and the fact it had to be managed from different cultural traditions meant that a particular piece of land was often claimed by the customary authorities of different communities. Boundaries between cultures were fluid and constantly changing, and limits of power were often contested and in flux,[1] in stark contradiction to the tribal identities as they were perceived and referred to when colonialism was established: culture was identified with race, and it was assumed that people sharing a culture by definition were organized in internally homogeneous political units. Furthermore, it was taken for granted that it was possible to distinguish a hierarchy between cultures and ethnic communities.[2] Switching back and forth between cultures and cultural identities often was the norm rather than the exception.[3]

An important development in the region of Lake Kivu in the last decades before colonization was the development of a strong and expansive state in Rwanda under Kigeri Rwabugiri, who was king of Rwanda from 1865 to 1895. He organized the state, established an administration and gave it a standardized structure of provinces, districts, hills and neighbourhoods administered by a hierarchy of chiefs. But Kigeri IV is best known for his military campaigns against neighbouring societies, including in what is today Kivu. His military campaigns led to the acquisition of status and booty within Rwanda and consolidated power and hierarchy within the state. But despite the destruction wrought on the neighbouring countries, there were very few true conquests or permanent political annexations as a result.[4]

When the Conference of Berlin was held between November 1884 and February 1885 to regulate the colonial ambitions and claims of the different European countries, no European eyes had ever seen Lake Kivu. Rwanda was assigned to the German empire, and Congo fell under the control of the Belgian King Leopold II and became the Congo Free State. The Germans and the CFS disputed the exact frontier for ages as the result of the arbitrary mapping of political boundaries in 'unexplored' territory.

Mathys concludes:

> the artificiality of this border did not lie in the fact that it separated people having established different links (be it family ties, ethnic, cultural or political links), but in the fact that in the frontier it meant a departure from a fluid and itinerant territoriality, in which alliances to different political centres were possible and subject to change, to a fixed form in which limits were more or less unchangeable and allegiances to different political centres were no longer tolerated.[5]

The result was the 'territorialization' of ethnicity.[6]

Parallel to the complex network of diverse but overlapping customary mechanisms of dealing with land, colonization introduced a more formal statutory system of land tenure under which land increasingly became a saleable good, something which was totally opposed to how land was perceived by the communities that actually lived on it. The dichotomy between customary and statutory systems was further complicated by the political and administrative organization the colonial state gave to its colony by creating new territories, chiefdoms and *groupements* separated by fluid boundaries. The Belgian scholar Jean-Claude Willame wrote that 'this colonial territorialisation planted the first seeds of future conflicts and crises'.[7] A second complication was the fact that the Belgians brought in people from outside the region to work on the land, primarily on plantations.[8] This migration that the Belgian colonial government used for providing labour to the ailing plantation economy in the Kivus (often through the use of force) was also used by Rwandan migrants in search of better living conditions.

This created a dichotomy between communities referred to as 'local' or 'native', as opposed to newcomers who were seen as 'migrants' or 'foreigners'. In the case of eastern Congo, most of these were Hutu from Rwanda. This created a permanent tension between native and migrant communities over the status of land occupied by the migrants and competition over power balances, demographically and politically, in the newly created administrative units.

The repressive and relatively strong colonial state managed to keep these tensions under control reasonably well. The regular outbursts of violence surrounding control over territory disappeared in the early stages of colonization. But the fragile post-colonial state was much less capable of dealing with land issues. As the curse of corruption became the regulating principle of the state during Mobutu's reign, the risks increased that the traditional leaders, supposed to take care of the land on behalf of the community, monetized parts of it in their own interest, thus contributing to a process of rapid privatization and alienation of land which became the property of powerful individuals or enterprises linked to the Zairian elite.[9]

Another important post-colonial development was the fact that democracy became an issue. Not that the country became democratic, but more than ever before the weight of a community was counted in numbers. Size did matter: political power was increasingly interlinked with the demographic balances within the different administrative divisions at all levels. Demographic importance as a basis for political representation in many cases intensified tensions between communities or gave communities the feeling of being marginalized.[10] In his excellent: 'North Kivu. The background to conflict in North Kivu province in eastern Congo', Jason Stearns analyses how the Hunde community was marginalized on what they considered as their ancestral land in the territories of Masisi and describes how a feeling of alienation and lack of political representation contributed to the community's perceived need to create its own armed group.[11] The absence of a functioning state as a regulator gave many Hunde the feeling they had no other option.

The land insecurity and the spoliation of the rural population heightened tensions between the 'native' population and the 'Banyarwanda' in Kivu. The integration of Rwandans and to a lesser extent Burundians in eastern Congo as a labour force to work on the colonial plantations had been preceded and followed by other waves of migration as a result of famine or conflict. After independence, the Banyarwanda elite attempted to acquire land in North Kivu as part of their economic survival strategy. Being outsiders to the complex network of traditional mechanisms of land management, they considered buying land through the statutory land law of 1973 as their only possibility to be independent from the customary authorities of the native communities and avoid paying taxes to them. Thus they acquired more than 90% of the former colonial plantation in the territories of Masisi and Rutshuru.

The Banyarwanda elite, politicians as well as businessmen, were well positioned in Mobutu's inner circle. It was under their influence, and particularly the president's cabinet chief Barthélemy Bisengimana, that Mobutu passed in 1972 the Law on Nationality, giving Zairian citizenship to anyone who had immigrated before 1960. For Mobutu the law was basically a tool to buy the loyalty of the Banyarwanda, whose support was necessary to impose his reign in the eastern provinces. The law formalized and accelerated the community's access to local economic resources and thus provoked the resentment of the local communities' elite. In 1981, some years after Bisengimana's fall, the law was changed again and citizenship became once more dependent upon descent from an ethnic group found within the borders of Zaire on 1 August 1885.[12] This is the moment the Kinyarwanda-speaking community from South Kivu started to refer to themselves as Banyamulenge – children of Mulenge, in the highlands of South Kivu – as a statement that their ancestors had been present on Zairian soil since the nineteenth century. On this basis, they claimed Zairian nationality and distinguished themselves from the Banyarwanda from North Kivu who descended from Rwandan immigrants and refugees in the twentieth century.[13] The result of juggling with the laws was that nationality and citizenship became highly politicized and sensitive, a matter often used as a political tool and divide-and-rule measure within Mobutu's inner circle.

The immediate consequence of the 1981 revision of the Nationality Law was not only that the Banyarwanda's nationality was in question, but it also cut off their elite's access to political power and reduced their right to buy land. The controversy paralysed, or at least slowed down, political life for more than a decade: the 1987 elections were not held because of the nationality question, and in 1991, at the opening of the *Conférence Nationale Souveraine* (CNS), Kinyarwanda-speakers were rejected as delegates because of their dubious nationality.

In the meantime, on 24 April 1990, Mobutu announced the multiparty state. Immediately new political parties mushroomed all over the country, many of them created along ethnic or regional lines with leaders who developed a populist discourse which further polarized the tensions related to identity.[14]

As part of the democratization process, new elections were scheduled and, as had been the case in 1987, Mobutu wanted to organize a census to identify nationalities prior to the elections. In 1991, the government in Kinshasa declared that it would not grant citizenship to immigrants (referred to as 'the transplanted' in colonial language, '*les transplantés*') or to their children. This declaration immediately stirred up unrest. Many registration offices were burned down by Banyarwanda gangs.[15] The census was cancelled and the multiparty elections planned by the CNS never took place.

This was the start of a rapid militarization of the communities that organized themselves in self-defence groups which started to dominate the province of North Kivu in the following years. The Nande were the first to have deployable militia in 1991, which they called Mai Mai. The name was used as a label for most similar self-defence groups in eastern Congo. Soon the Hunde, the Nyanga and the Tembo also had their own Mai Mai groups ready to fight with the Banyarwanda militia. Violence intensified in 1993, first in Walikale and then in Masisi, Rutshuru and Walikale. In that year alone 20,000 people died because of the clashes, and 200,000 people were displaced by the violence.[16] Mobutu's disintegrating state was totally unable to intervene locally. A few months later, as a consequence of the Rwandan genocide, two million Hutu refugees arrived in Kivu, including the Interahamwe and the former Rwandan army, the main slaughterers in the genocide. The local conflicts in Kivu became part of a regional downward spiral which soon was to give birth to the Great African War.[17]

Bucyalimwe Mararo developed an interesting case: he described the relationship between land, power and conflict in Muvunyi-Kibabisi, a rural area in Masisi, between 1940 and 1994.[18] Muvunyi-Kibabisi's approximate extent is 336 km² and, according to the 1983 census, 41,631 people: 30,507 Hutu, 7,258 Tutsi, 3,724 Hunde, eighty-seven Twa and fifty-five others reside there.

Mararo examines how the Belgian administration applied the divide-and-rule policy even at this micro-level in order to protect colonial interests and failed to establish a framework that could facilitate ethnic harmony in the area. Until the end of the 1930s, Muvunyi-Kibabiw was still covered by forest and underpopulated. Twa and Hunde families were scattered throughout the forest and enjoyed vast land resources. These were reduced to a minimal level with the settlement of white and Rwandan populations in the area in the 1940s and 1950s. The colonial state expropriated lands from the Twa and Hunde to benefit white and Rwandan immigrants, but colonial control over Hutu and Tutsi was exercised through Hunde customary chiefs.

An agro-farming economy emerged, with cash crops growing on white plantations and food crops on African (mostly Hutu) plots of land. Hunter-gatherer economies disappeared completely, while

Hunde and Twa were integrated into a farm economy but with few land resources. In addition to both food and cash crops, the white settlers developed an interest in raising cattle, and mixed farming became the dominant form of the economy by the late 1950s.

The political status of immigrants was not clearly defined while their settlement was considered definitive. The immigrants were landowners, but politically subordinate to Hunde authority, which kept them implicitly in a tenancy status. The Hunde never gave up the idea of being landowners and the immigrants never considered themselves mere land users. In the first years after independence, more than 80% of elected local counsellors in Masisi were Rwandan immigrants. They did not run for office at the provincial and national level because of the absence of well-educated and politically aware individuals. Their Hunde rivals profited from the situation and rose to top positions at provincial and central level.

When Mobutu installed the one-party state, he appointed Hunde as local MPR leaders. In the first years after independence, white farmers were leaving the country. This was the end of the cash crop era and cattle farming started to expand. Hunde party and official representatives took advantage of their positions to strengthen their position in rural life. Land expropriation became common, and holding power was a key path to land acquisition. Hunde struggled to establish and maintain a monopoly on power and tried to expel Hutu and Tutsi from the area in order to control their settled lands. On the other hand, Hutu and Tutsi struggled to participate in the political process. Land conflicts became more frequent and in the 1980s more than 90% of the conflicts brought to court related to land. The relations between Hutu and Tutsi deteriorated through suspicion and intrigue.

In the last years of Mobutu's reign, local reactions to the new situation followed ethnic lines. Hunde, afraid to lose their monopoly on power in democratic elections, tried, in alliance with other ethnic groups of North Kivu (Nande, Nyanga, Tembo), to exclude Rwandan immigrants from the National Conference. The political status of Rwandan immigrants was not seriously discussed. They were considered as foreigners. But the CNS ended when in July 1994 two million Rwandan Hutu arrived in North and South Kivu and history took an entirely new turn.

Four different groups of Kinyarwanda-speakers have to be distinguished: (1) those 'native' to Congo (Hutu and Tutsi) in the region around Rutshuru, as well as groups such as Banyamulenge, who probably came in the nineteenth century (but at this time people of all cultures moved around quite a lot); (2) migrants who came between 1937 and the 1950s in the wake of a Belgian resettlement scheme (but also a continuation of older patterns of mobility); (3) those who fled 'social revolution' in Rwanda between 1959 and 1963 (mainly Tutsi, for example around Nyabibwe and Ihula); and (4) the Hutu refugees of 1994.

The land issue, and the way it is interlinked with identity, is extremely complex and has an important impact on Kivu's conflicts and on the possibilities of solving them. The land issue has made the peasants of Kivu extremely vulnerable. I have discussed the dualism between customary and contemporary legislation. Peasants depend on customary law and are swept away in a context where access to land is no longer regulated by customary oral contracts but through land registration procedures and the issuing of land titles in a monetized circuit which favours the political and urban economic elite. Small producers are losing the land they have occupied for generations and they often have no other option but to lease land from big landowners. The land available for peasants has decreased dramatically over recent decades while the demographic pressures continue to increase. This process of commercialization and privatization of land has marginalized peasants in Kivu and elsewhere in Congo. It not only deprived them of an economic base, it also contributed to the fact that they are scarcely represented in national and provincial political institutions. This means that the voices of 70% to 80% of the people are not heard in public debate.

The development of the land issue hollowed out the power and legitimacy of the customary authorities. At the local level, in the *chefferies*, *groupements* and villages, customary leaders exercise state authority. But they depend on (and are sometimes in competition with) the local state administration, which is not customary. The first prerogative of customary authorities is to decide who has the right to exploit which land and for how long. The privatization of land reduced their power. In a first phase, many of them earned a lot of money by selling land. Later, impoverished and without any vacant plots to sell, the customary leaders often sell the same plot of land several times to several people, thus causing land disputes that are often difficult to resolve.[19] Customary power has been a recognized political institution in Congo with a formal role to play at the local level since independence. Like all other political institutions in Congo, it is eroded by clientelism and corruption. Customary power is also complicated because it is deeply rooted in an ethnic environment and therefore liable to interpersonal, interfamily and inter-clan relations. When a local chief dies, succession is often controversial and subject to rival networks which sometimes deeply divide the community.

Ethnic and cultural identities of individuals and groups are not fixed categories. However, although they might usually be fluid, they have a tendency to become fixed in times of conflict. Conflicts between communities often develop an identity-related dimension, especially when they are linked to land and power. Local politicians frequently use ethnicity as a lever to mobilize an electorate. The 'indigenousness' of the people they want to stigmatize can be questioned in order to delegitimize them. In many areas of eastern Congo, such politicians focus on communities which have resulted from successive waves of migration from the neighbouring countries. But not always: such arguments are also used against communities whose alleged roots lie in other parts of Congo. But essential in this discourse is that people from communities that are considered newcomers are denied rights, including those related to land. The close connection between identity and land issues in an environment under heavy demographic pressure is at the root of many disputes and conflicts in the Great Lakes region.

The Mutarule massacre

Let us have a look at a concrete case[20] where issues about identity, land and customary authorities have intermingled with the recent wars and transboundary conflicts. On the evening of Friday 6 June 2014, at least thirty-three unarmed Congolese civilians were killed in and around the village of Mutarule, on the plains of the Ruzizi river, 9 km from Sange, between Uvira and Bukavu. The minister of communication and spokesman of the Congolese government, Lambert Mende, called the incident a revenge attack by the community of a cattle herder killed during an attempt to steal cows belonging to another farmer. The victims (eight children, seventeen women and eight men) belonged to the ethnic community of the Bafuliro.[21]

The area around the Ruzizi is very conflict prone, not only because of the cohabitation between farmers and livestock-breeders, but also because of the proximity of borders. Between Bukavu and Kamanyola the river Ruzizi separates Rwanda from Congo, and from Kamanyola to Gatumba the river is the border between Congo and Burundi. On the evening of Saturday 7 June, the UN Mission in DR Congo MONUSCO issued a statement saying that 'fierce fighting' had taken place the night before between the Bafuliro on one side and the Barundi and Banyamulenge on the other.

The biggest source of conflict on the Ruzizi plains in recent years has been the killing of the chief of the administrative unit (the *chefferie*) in April 2012. Since the colonial period, the Barundi and the Bafuliro have shared this *chefferie* and have lived in permanent competition over the control of land for farming and grazing. The cohabitation of the two communities is complicated by the fact that the Bafuliro are considered to be autochthonous Congolese, while the Barundi, who have lived in Congo since at least the early nineteenth century, are related to the people on the other side of the border and also speak Kirundi. They are considered by many to be foreigners.

In 1928 the territory of Uvira was divided into three *chefferies*: one ruled by the Bavira, one by the Bafuliro and one by the Barundi. By granting each a *chefferie*, the Belgians gave them the customary rights to the land. The Bafuliro contested this several times during and also after independence. The tensions and competition between the two communities became sharpened by poverty and under-development, by poor management of land issues and by the governance crisis caused by the absence of the state at a local level. This absence created a lot of space for a customary chief (*mwami*) whose role is important but rather vaguely described in the laws.[22]

In 1996, Mwami Ndagaboye of the Barundi was deposed by Laurent Kabila's advancing AFDL. He went into exile but came back in 1998 as an RCD officer. For the Bafuliro, choosing to side with a rebellion against the DRC government meant that he lost legitimacy as *mwami* of the *chefferie*. In 2004, the government in Kinshasa formalized the position of a Mufuliro[23] as customary chief. For the Bafuliro community, this decision terminated what they had previously considered to be an absurdity: being ruled by foreigners.

In the years after 2004, the Mufuliro customary chief was increasingly criticized, particularly within his own community, for his mismanagement of matters related to land. Early in 2012 he was dismissed from his office by the minister of the interior and customary affairs and Kinshasa decided to reinstall Mwami Ndabagoye. This decision took control over the *chefferie* away from the Bafuliro and gave it back to the Barundi, triggering a new wave of inter-community violence in the months after the troubled elections of November 2011. On 25 April 2012, on the eve of his reinstallation as customary chief, Mwami Ndabagoye was killed. His death intensified violence in the region. A code of conduct between the two communities was facilitated by the government but it was not able to reconcile Bafuliro and Barundi, or to restore stability.

The area is also vulnerable to conflict because of the difficult cohabitation between agriculturalists and pastoralists, especially during the transhumance period (the seasonal movement of people with their livestock). Transhumance itself can become a source of conflict: not only does the passage of herds often cause damage to the farmers' crops, it also touches on the sensitive area of access to and control of land. The cohabitation between pastoralists and agriculturalists used to be regulated by traditional institutions, through a tenure system uniting land applicants and land managers.

But these institutions have been dismantled by war: the emergence of guns and armed groups undermined the space for non-violent settlement of cattle-related conflict. Farmers use weapons to prevent herders from accessing pastures, and herders use them to force access to pastures. People are regularly killed – the question in such cases is always how to manage the situation so that the incident remains between individuals, rather than becoming an issue between communities.

But what happened on 6 June on the Ruzizi plains is probably not directly linked to transhumance either. Some sources on the ground consider the massacre to have been a reaction from the Banyamulenge – the Tutsi community of South Kivu – to a series of kidnappings and killings of members of their community, including an army colonel. One day prior to the massacre, a Munyamulenge herder was killed and decapitated during a cattle raid. It is still unclear which individuals were responsible for the massacre and what exactly the role was of Banyamulenge soldiers or the military hierarchy.

I often pass through Mutarule, which is on the way from Bukavu to Bukumbura, and the shadow of the massacre still hangs over the area. Local people have no doubt about what really happened on 6 and 7 June 2014:

Twenty Banyamulenge soldiers have left Bukavu and drove with jeeps to Mutarule to take revenge on behalf of General Masunzu, then military commander of the FARDC in South

Kivu, because one of his shepherds had been killed and some dozens of his cows were stolen.[24]

The case is dramatic but also interesting, because many dimensions of the conflicts afflicting eastern Congo come together: the land and identity issues of course; the explosive cohabitation of 'autochthonous' and 'foreign' communities; the failed attempts to create a truly unified army; the apparently unsolvable problem of the armed groups; and the uneasy coexistence of a non-operational local administration and contested customary authorities.

Conclusion

Recent decades have placed layer upon layer of conflict on top of an ancient and complex puzzle of communities with historical bonds and divisions, where identity issues overlap with conflict regarding land. The violence, especially since the start of the wars in 1996, has been responsible for the deaths of millions of people, devastating local economies, infrastructure and social coherence. The trivialization of violence and the emergence of armed groups has affected the traditional structures of society, changing the economy from a parallel, informal economy to a war economy. In this way, conflict at a grassroots level plays a part in other conflicts, forming a complex mixture of conflicts with provincial, national and regional dimensions. One of the main dramas of the DRC is that this complexity has never been fully understood by the international partners and the donor community, and even by Congo's political elite in Kinshasa, so that programmes were designed and solutions proposed that took a top-down approach, which ultimately meant they were condemned to lack impact.

Chapter 3

THE ELECTIONS OF 2006

A phoenix not arising from its ashes

The Great African War ended with a tough set of negotiations under intense international surveillance, and agreements which, rather than reconciling water and fire, put them together in a transitional government. The partners in this shaky construction had little confidence in each other and still less in the chances that the procedure would lead to peace and democracy. The international supervision was so strict that many started to consider it as a form of guardianship. Even if it didn't bring peace, though, it changed the open war into a low-intensity conflict, and the transitional government was able to organize elections in 2006 (one-and-a-half years later than the agreed date), which Congolese and international observers proclaimed reasonably free and fair.

On 17 December 2002, the Global and All-Inclusive Agreement was signed in Pretoria between the different parties that had started the Inter-Congolese Dialogue ten months earlier in Sun City. The signatories agreed to install a transitional government where, at all levels, mandates and responsibilities were divided between the formally warring (Kabila's government, RCD-Goma, MLC, RCD-K Mouvement de Libération, Mai Mai) or non-warring parties (the unarmed opposition and civil society). This division started at the presidency, because Kabila had to share the presidential space with four vice-presidents: Jean-Pierre Bemba, the flamboyant leader of the MLC, Azarias Ruberwa, who had gradually managed to take political control of RCD-Goma, the former key collaborator of Father Kabila Abdoulaye Yerodia on behalf of the government and, after a tough competition, Arthur Z'ahidi Ngoma as representative of the opposition. This configuration gave the formula its name: 1+4, 'something that the institutional international community was ecstatic about but that other, more seasoned observers disbelievingly looked upon as some kind of a monster'.[1]

The transitional government was eventually operational on 1 July 2003 and had a mandate of two years. Its mission was to re-establish governmental authority throughout the Congolese territory, to establish national reconciliation, to integrate the combatants of all rebellions, militias and other armed groups into one disciplined, efficient army, and, most of all, to organize free and fair elections. But the rivalry and suspicion between the different partners was so great that the government had serious difficulties making real progress, to the extent that people in the streets of Kinshasa and elsewhere very soon started to make jokes about the unworkable construction and refer to it as 1+4=0.

In the meantime, the RCD-Goma and the MLC were reorganizing themselves as political parties. Kabila established his own party, the *Parti du Peuple pour la Reconstruction et la Démocratie* (PPRD). A key personality in this process was Vital Kamerhe, who became minister of information and later secretary-general of the PPRD.[2]

Five new institutions were created in support of democracy, each with a civil servant representative as president. The Observatory for Human Rights, the Truth and Reconciliation Commission and the Commission 'Ethics and the Struggle against Corruption' would never play a major role in the transition. The High Authority for Media, presided over by journalist and founder of the newspaper *Le Potentiel*, Modeste Mutinga, took on a higher profile, but a leading role was reserved for the independent electoral commission, CEI (*Commission Electorale Indépendante*). Its president was Reverend Apollinaire Malumalu, a Catholic priest, Rector of Graben University in Butembo and a civil society activist on (among other issues) natural resources.

The international community was granted an institutional and formalized role through the CIAT anticipated in the constitution of the transition as the emanation of the Congolese will to involve its international partners in the peace process. But several observers considered it an instrument of international tutelage[3] and in any case 'a parallel executive body heavily involved in elaborating strategies and policies relating to political, economic and security priorities'.[4]

The second pillar of the international accompaniment of the peace process was MONUC, whose military strength was nearly doubled to almost 11,500 soldiers during the transition. Though important for their dissuasive impact on potential spoilers of the peace process, they were heartily hated by nearly everybody in eastern Congo as people did not feel protected by the UN Mission, despite the fact that protection of civilians was a prominent part of its mandate. The mission was not much present in the field and not at all proactive, with a rather vague role and too little coordination between its different structures. MONUC's brigades were often absent at the time and place violence occurred and the mission's chain of command was sometimes intersected or even overruled by the capitals of the brigades' home countries. On top of this were cases of serious misbehaviour and criminal activities on the part of individual UN soldiers, such as sexual violence or involvement in the illicit traffic of natural resources. The result was that the Congolese citizens and the UN Mission which had come to protect them in effect lived on two different planets. Many Congolese and foreign observers had high hopes for a more efficient UN Mission in the DRC when former US ambassador William Swing replaced the Cameroonian diplomat Amos Namanga Ngongi in July 2003 as the Special Representative of the UN Secretary-General and the head of MONUC. Swing had a higher, more proactive profile[5] but, at least in the eyes of the Congolese population, this did not make enough difference to justify the huge costs of MONUC.

The foreign armies had already left the country in the months before the transition, and security improved in most parts of eastern Congo, although the 'fire of conflict would not burn out quite so fast'.[6] Especially in Ituri, the violence continued as if there were no peace process at all. The armed groups from Ituri had never signed the Pretoria Peace Agreement, although they were part of the demobilization programme and were on the list to be integrated into the new army. But seven armed groups, with approximately 15,000 soldiers combined, continued to fight for control over border posts and mining sites. The violence increased in December 2004, and at the end of February 2005 nine blue helmets from Bangladesh were killed.[7]

In Kivu, most of the armed groups decreased their activities but their demobilization, disarmament and reintegration progressed very slowly and most of the groups were never dismantled. The FDLR remained present and powerful in North and South Kivu. They were the remnants of the Rwandan army under Habyarimana and the Hutu militias who were responsible for the genocide, and had been able to maintain their structure, armoury and even administration. They functioned as a well-organized conventional army with ranks, uniforms, administration and leaves of absence.[8] They actually paid their combatants, something that could not be said about the Congolese regular army. Throughout the years of its presence in Kivu, the FDLR has transformed itself into a rather successful economic enterprise based on illicit trade and imposing taxes on the Congolese civilian population. Charcoal extraction, mainly from the Virunga Park, is big business in North Kivu, with profits up to $2.5 million a year.[9] Other important economic activities are poaching (including illegal fishing), the gold trade and the exploitation of timber and hemp. But the most important source of income for FDLR is taxation imposed on the population. To deploy these lucrative activities, FDLR has developed over the years a network of complex relationships and complicities with local and provincial authorities, other armed groups, the business community on both sides of all the borders and with key commanders in the Congolese and Rwandan security services.[10]

The most difficult moment of the transition was the insurgency of Laurent Nkunda in May and June 2004. Nkunda was an RCD-Goma officer who had never joined the transition and stayed behind in Kivu with the nucleus of a new Tutsi rebellion, the CNDP. He was one of the commanders in charge of the RCD-Goma troops that were responsible for the massacres in Kisangani in 2002,[11] and he was still trusted by Rwanda at a moment when it had started to doubt the loyalty of the entire RCD-Goma leadership. Since the rebel movement had joined the transition, Kigali no longer took for granted that its leadership would automatically serve the interests of their former donors. So Nkunda was kept behind as a military plan B in case the transition and the elections turned out to be disastrous for Rwanda.

The insurgency started with tensions within the newly integrated military structure in South Kivu between the commander General Nabyolwa, who had served in the war under Kabila, and the former RCD-Goma officer Jules Mutebutsi. It developed into an open conflict with violent incidents on 26 May eventually motivating Laurent Nkunda to enter Bukavu with 2,500 soldiers, mainly Tutsi from Rutshuru. Nkunda took Bukavu on 29 May and in the following days his troops terrorized the city with door-to-door looting and rapes.[12] This behaviour, of course, discredited Nkunda even more in international public opinion. Apparently, taking Bukavu was not the result of extensive strategic anticipation and once the city was in his hands Nkunda didn't seem to know what to do next.[13] Eventually he pulled out on 4 June after a negotiation with MONUSCO and withdrew with his men into the forests of Masisi.[14]

Ten weeks later, on 13 August, 160 Banyamulenge were killed in a refugee camp in Gatumba, between Uvira and Bujumbura, a few yards on the Burundian side of the border. The Burundian Hutu rebel *Forces Nationales de Libération* (FNL) claimed the attack but there were many indications that they had carried out the massacre together with FDLR and some fanatically anti-Tutsi Mai Mai groups.

Both events weighed heavily on the transition. Not only were the incidents polarized between Kinyarwanda-speaking and 'autochthonous' communities, thus between RCD-Goma and the government camp, but they also had a very negative impact on the already fragile cohesion within RCD-Goma. Yet it lived on 'with its troubled former battlefield areas that it was never able to fully pacify',[15] without establishing the state's control over the entire territory and without improving the human rights situation, public finances or economic governance.

Eventually the elections did take place. Not in June 2005, but more than a year later. Kabila stepped into the ring leading a regional and ethnic-based coalition, the *Alliance de la Majorité Présidentielle* (AMP). He won the first round on 30 July 2006 with 44.81%. As a consequence a second round was necessary against Jean-Pierre Bemba, who obtained 20.03% of the votes. A few weeks later, heavy fighting broke out around Bemba's TV station and residence, when zealots from Kabila's camp tried to provoke incidents that would justify the cancellation of the second round and lead to the winner being proclaimed immediately. Twenty-three people died and forty-three were wounded between 20 and 23 August.[16]

Kabila formed a coalition with the third and fourth placed candidates in the first round, the old Lumumbist icon Antoine Gizenga and former president Mobutu's son Nzanga. On October 2006, Kabila beat Bemba with 58.05% of the vote against 40.95%. On 6 December 2006 Kabila was sworn in as the first elected president of the Third Republic.

The parliament was terribly fragmented. Kabila's PPRD had won 111 seats (21%) and Bemba's MLC sixty-four (13%), eleven parties had between seven and thirty-four seats, forty-three parties won one or two seats but obtained as a (very heterogeneous) group 11% of the parliamentary mandates. The legislative mosaic was completed by sixty-three independents – a fluid mass of customary chiefs, successful businessmen and former warlords – rooted in local reality but generally without any particular political view or a social project worthy of its name. Many people were sceptical about the micro-parties or the independents, and did not expect them to do much more than sit and wait to sell their vote when someone was prepared to pay a decent price for it.[17] Tshisekedi's UDPS had boycotted the elections and remained outside the parliament.

An important feature of the election at all levels was its regional and ethnic dimension: the lack of social security institutions leaves citizens dependent on their regional, social, religious and ethnic communities and thus inclines voters to favour candidates sympathetic to their groups. This was also the case of Kabila: he owed his victory to his overwhelming success in the three parts of the historical Kivu province (South and North Kivu and Maniema), Katanga, where his late father was born, and the Swahili-speaking half of Province Orientale. The western provinces had massively voted for Bemba.

The direct elections as a whole went smoothly and were declared free and fair by all independent observers, but the indirect elections (the election of senators and the nomination of the governors and vice-governors) made clear that despite the achievements of the electoral process, a democratic culture had yet to develop in Congo. Votes and mandates were negotiated and bought almost openly. The local elections were not organized at all, which gave Congo's institutional architecture something like a palace with a heavy roof but no walls. Theodore Trefon concluded that the 'democratization' process had progressed because of the pressure of the international community, but that the realities and practices on the ground had made clear that democracy had been adapted to the logics and rigours of clientelism instead of the other way around.[18]

In February 2007, Kabila appointed Antoine Gizenga as his prime minister, but the new government had huge difficulties operationalizing the institutions of the Third Republic. The political constellation was fragile, since the political landscape crystallized around strong personalities and weak parties. The PPRD's tendency to dominate the AMP created a lot of frustrations within the majority. The population perceived the inaction of the government in eastern Congo as a huge disappointment. After all, they had elected Kabila because he had put an end to the war and unified the country. But he wasn't able to wipe out the pockets of violence, which kept the country in a state of low-intensity conflict. His popularity dropped dramatically.[19]

Neither Kabila nor Gizenga managed to show convincing leadership, while ministers were not really controlling their own departments as most of the important decisions were taken within the circles of influence around Kabila's office. Ultimately, the country was governed by a small group of people around Kabila. The central personality was Augustin Katumba Mwanke, Kabila's own Rasputin who could make or break people in the presidential sphere. He strictly controlled who had access to the president's ear and who didn't, and was also the man with the key to the state's cash box.

Vital Kamerhe was another crucial figure. He had worked with Mzee Kabila and later became a close friend to Joseph. He had played an important role in Kabila's campaign as one of the few people who were fluent in Congo's four official national languages: Kikongo, Lingala, Tshiluba and Kiswahili. Kabila rewarded Kamerhe for his work as well as for his own overwhelming electoral victory as MP in Bukavu by giving him one of the most prestigious positions in the Third Republic: the speaker of Parliament.

John Numbi was also important to Kabila, with whom he shares his province of origin and ethnic community. They are both Balubakat from northern Katanga. In the early 1990s he was a militant in the Katangese movement who organized the ethnic purification of the inhabitants of the province with roots in the Kasai. He joined Laurent Kabila's uprising in 1997 and in 2001 was appointed commander of the Congolese air force. In July 2007 he became national chief of the police.

A fourth very influential individual was Samba Kaputo, who was born in Katanga but grew up in South Kivu. He had an impressive academic and political career and later became an important advisor to both Kabilas. He died in August 2007.

These four people had mentored Kabila after his father's death. With their help he managed to remove the hawks from Mzee's entourage, put the peace process back on track and organize a successful campaign. The configuration of this small nucleus reveals how important the provinces of Katanga and South Kivu were in the establishment of the reign of both Kabilas. They ruled the country with and through Kabila after the elections in 2006. A second circle of influence, a bit more distant from the epicentre of power, contains people such as Marcelin Chisambo, Evariste Boshab, Adolphe Lumanu, Antoine Ghonda, Pierre Lumbi and some others.

Bemba never took up his role as leader of the opposition. Relations with Kabila and the army remained very tense after his electoral defeat and the violent confrontations in Kinshasa in August 2006. Bemba refused to dismantle the personal guards he had as vice-president during the transition and did not integrate them into the regular army. This explosive situation developed into a new crisis, and on 22 March 2007 Kabila's presidential guards attacked Bemba's guards in La Gombe, the administrative, political and commercial heart of Kinshasa. Bemba abandoned his men and found refuge in the South African embassy. He left Congo on 11 April and settled in Portugal where his family had property. On 24 May 2008 he was arrested in Brussels on the basis of an international warrant from the International Criminal Court (ICC), charged with crimes against humanity and war crimes during his campaign in the Central African Republic to support former president Ange-Félix Patassé. On 21 March 2016, Jean-Pierre Bemba was found guilty of rape, murder and pillage, and three months later received a sentence of eighteen years. This judgment was an important victory from a human rights perspective, but many Bemba supporters considered the trial highly politicized and biased.

The Third Republic started off with a highly fragmented parliament, a rather powerless government that did not try too hard to overcome its own inertness and a barely existing opposition in the form of the UDPS – which remained outside the institutions and the debate due to its refusal to participate in the elections – and Jean-Pierre Bemba, who had left the country.

The first legislature of the Democratic Republic of Congo's Third Republic proved difficult: some of the institutions were never installed. Local elections, for instance, never took place. Others were, but functioned with a noticeable democratic deficit. Despite much rhetoric surrounding the '*cinq chantiers*'[20] which formed the heart of Kabila's 2006 election campaign, nothing much seemed to happen. The president had promised spectacular improvements on infrastructure, jobs, education, health, water and electricity, but few Congolese citizens saw tangible improvements in their daily living conditions. Furthermore, Kabila, who had been elected because he had brought an end to the war, failed to address issues of insecurity and impunity.

In the end, Joseph Kabila did not manage to reinvent the Congolese state. Like his predecessors, he governed through a patrimonial system with a very small inner circle and a large network of local, national and international stakeholders. As a result, Congo remained a very weak state in a condition of ruin. In *Congo Masquerade*, Theodore Trefon describes how the mechanism worked:

> In the arena of Congolese politics and international relations, masquerade is played out by local actors to obscure, dissimulate or camouflage their real objectives. International players play the same game for similar reasons. Congolese authorities cunningly smother reform initiatives but without completely suffocating them. The twofold objective is to keep them alive (for funding, to maintain tolerable relations with foreign partners or to stay on board as part of a process). At the same time, they manoeuvre to slow down, block or sabotage reform.[21]

One of the domains where there was very little progress was the decentralization process. The main reason for this was that the organization of local elections was not considered a priority. Congo has struggled since independence with the balance between central government and the provincial authorities, which is probably not surprising for a multi-ethnic country the size of Western Europe with internal boundaries designed by colonial administrators. The question had already arisen in the heated debate between federalists and 'unitarists' in the months leading up to the transfer of power from the colonial to the independent state, and led to the implosion of Congo shortly after Independence Day. When Mobutu took power on 24 November 1965, he established a centralized dictatorship. Existing provinces were reduced to a purely administrative role and lost their relatively high level of autonomy.[22] The Constitution of 2006 foresaw the division of the eleven existing provinces into twenty-six provinces. Kivu was not to be part of this process because the historical Kivu province had already been divided into three new provinces (North Kivu, South Kivu and Maniema) in 1988. The constitution foresaw elected assemblies at different levels (districts, communes, *secteurs* and *chefferies*) but not at the level of the *territoires*. According to the constitution, 40% of central revenue was to be allocated to the provinces, while other legislation relates to the definition of locally raised revenue and how it is to be distributed. Altogether 10% of all state revenues was to be channelled into a dedicated fund to finance projects and programmes in decentralized areas as a means of fostering national solidarity.

In principle, decentralization should have consolidated democracy from below by creating a framework for participative governance, helping to reconstruct the state and restore its credibility. It could have been a school for democracy where citizens learnt how democracy works, and facilitated the renewal of the political landscape with the emergence of new leadership. But that didn't happen. Decentralization remained no more than a concept defined in the Constitution of the Third Republic, which continued to function as a federal-type structure. The 2006 elections created provincial assemblies, but the process of bringing accountability and citizen control to the grassroots level as a way to strengthen responsible governance from below did not go any further than that.[23] And very soon it became clear that the provincial assemblies had a huge problem of capacity, integrity and even a proper understanding of their own role.

In the aftermath of the 2006 elections, Joseph Kabila continued to lead the country as head of state. There was a lot of speculation about his ability to hold that office. He remained enigmatic, silent as a sphinx and very inaccessible except to his immediate collaborators. He had impressed a lot of people in the first years of his presidency. Very few people knew him when he succeeded his father, but in a few months he had managed to form a government without the influential hardliners from his father's administration, and had put the peace process back on track. Later, some of his weaknesses became obvious. In the difficult year 2004, during the transition, Kabila failed to react effectively to a number of crisis situations, such as Nkunda occupying Bukavu and the massacre in Gatumba. Rumours were launched in this period about his alleged cocaine abuse and irresponsible behaviour, but there was no solid evidence that Kabila would not be able to play his role.

Following the elections, though, Kabila grew in confidence, spurred on by the fact he had won the first democratic elections in the DRC after decades of Mobutism, two wars and the subsequent complicated peace and transition period. Also the space around him was reorganized after the elections: Augustin Katumba Mwanke took a much more central position and all other key collaborators had to pass through him in order to gain access to Kabila.

Throughout his reign Kabila has shown he is not a good communicator and finds it difficult to reach a decision. When he is in doubt and under pressure, the process from thought to action appears to be: (1) there is some violent event or action; (2) withdraw into his shell for an interior battle while surrounded by collaborators and mandarins trying and failing to get through to him with alarmist messages; (3) after some (often a lot of) time, somebody says something that rouses him out of his silent lethargy and he starts to negotiate, often in a position of weakness because events have worsened during his period of silence. One of his collaborators told me: 'Now that we lost Katumba Mwanke, our young president has become a ship without a radar. He does not listen anymore to advice'.[24]

Immediately after his election as first president of the Third Republic, however, Kabila initially felt stronger than ever. One of his first priorities after taking office was to dismantle CIAT, drastically reduce the impact of the international community and discourage any form of multilateral approach. He preferred talking with his different partners on a bilateral basis rather than facing them as a group.

The 2006 elections were the apotheosis of the Western partners' engagement in the peace and democratization process, but they were side-lined almost immediately thereafter. The EU, for instance, was the proud godfather standing beside the cradle of the Third Republic. The Union and its member states had played an important role in CIAT; providing the large majority of the funds necessary to organize what were called the most expensive elections in the history of the planet. In addition, the EU had sent a military mission (EUFOR) to the DRC to help MONUC in securing the elections in Kinshasa, and also had the ambition of contributing to security sector reform (SSR) and the integration of the different armed groups into the regular army, FARDC (Forces Armées de la République Démocratique du Congo), mainly by controlling the chain of payments to the military, and modernizing both adminis-tration and human resources management.

Congo's Western partners had walked a delicate tightrope between loyal support and focused political pressure to keep the democratization process on the rails. But after the elections, with Kabila feeling legitimized and strong, he remained interested in the support but no longer took the pressure as seriously.

In September 2007, the Minister of Infrastructure Pierre Lumbi, president of the *Mouvement Social pour le Renouveau* (MSR), the biggest party of the presidential majority after Kabila's PPRD, announced that Congo had signed an important cooperation pact with the People's Republic of China. China committed to investing $9 billion in the president's five *chantiers* and $3 billion in the mining sector. The money would be provided by Chinese state-owned enterprises. A joint venture was set up with one-third of the shares in Congolese hands and two-thirds controlled by the Chinese partners. China's part of the deal entitled them to up to 10 million tons of copper and hundreds of thousands of tons of cobalt from Katanga. The contract stipulated that 0.5% of each project should go to training and transfer of technology, 1% to social works and 3% to cover the costs of the negative environmental impact of the project; 10% of the work had to be carried out by Congolese enterprises.[25]

The 'Chinese contract', as it was called, provoked great animosity in the Western embassies, and was almost considered an act of aggression. The three main arguments motivating the panic were: firstly, it was feared that the contract would be old wine in new bottles as far as the good old plundering of Congo's natural resources was concerned. Once again, Congo would be on the losing end of an unbalanced exchange. Secondly, because the deal was presented in the Western press as an impressive loan, it was seen as a disastrous route to building up a new insurmountable burden of national debt after decades of efforts by the International Monetary Fund (IMF) and World Bank to bring it under control. And thirdly, European and North American governments were concerned that the Chinese money would be a blank cheque to the untrustworthy Congolese authorities, in contrast to their own approach of using aid as a lever to achieve greater respect for human rights and better governance from the Congolese government. The Chinese, it was said, would not have these preoccupations. Aside from the fact that the Western record on plundering, debt, human rights and good governance throughout Congolese history do not give many reasons to justify an attitude of moral superiority, it was obvious that the uneasiness with China's new prominence was the result of a loss of space and leverage in the decision-making spheres of the country.[26]

International NGOs specializing in the domain of mining and natural resources management raised the question of transparency. The deal was negotiated behind closed doors, with Katumba Mwanke and Pierre Lumbi as key negotiators, was never discussed in Parliament and was kept out of sight of the ministries of finance, economy and budget. Absolutely no information was available to the public about fundamental financial aspects of the contract, such as the sale prices of minerals, and therefore there was a woeful lack of information on what infrastructure was to be built and at what cost. China had a very ambiguous position, with a potential conflict of interest in the fact that the Chinese state was likely be both buyer and principal seller of the minerals.[27]

In practice, the partnership with China took off rather cautiously. Neither the Chinese way of life nor corporate culture were a perfect match for the Congolese managers, clerks and labourers, and China had to learn how to deal with the traditional pitfalls of working with the Congolese state.[28] The cooperation was much more successful in the second half of the legislature, when the regime started to worry about presenting the results of the deal to the voters in order to be re-elected.

But the most important, direct and tangible impact of the Chinese contract was that it gave Kabila's self-confidence a boost and reinforced his position in the view of his electorate as well as on the international scene. He knew he no longer had to depend only on his traditional Western partners. It soon became clear that the Chinese interest was not an isolated phenomenon, but the most visible manifestation of a much larger process of globalization in a multi-polar world.

Maintaining a war economy after the war

Neither the transition nor the elections brought back peace in eastern Congo. After the withdrawal of foreign troops at the end of 2002 as part of the peace process, armed violence remained a part of everyday life in many areas of Kivu, committed by groups whose origins, structure, vision (if any) and objectives were very locally rooted, but whose impact remained global by the fact that they were one of the factors impeding the renaissance of the Congolese state and the return of the rule of law in eastern Congo.[29]

These included the Mai Mai groups, often splinter groups of larger units, which refused to be integrated into the army and rejected any form of authority. Small groups that had survived amid the debris of the war were no longer freedom fighters or defenders of an ideology, but social bandits whose motivation was basically economic. Their survival as actors on the scene was closely linked to failing disarmament, demobilization, repatriation, reintegration and resettlement (DDRRR)[30] and security sector reform[31] programmes.

The formation of a new unified and disciplined army to serve the country and protect the people produced very few convincing results, and the army remained the main source of human rights violations – in the years since they have remained more part of the problem than part of the solution.

The unification of the army did not progress as expected and the SSR's results were disproportionately small relative to the financial, human and other means invested in it by several bilateral and multilateral partners. There were several reasons why Congo did not manage to forge one army by assembling the different armed groups and small factions.

Firstly, there was and is a lack of political will, based on distrust in the process. A warlord or rebel leader will not have much desire to dismantle his entire military strength knowing he might need it on the day that the peace process is derailed.

Secondly, there were the logistics: dissolving an armed group involves receiving, registering and disarming every single militia member, sheltering and feeding them, training and organizing them in other units and then redeploying them. This process requires camps and barracks which barely existed in Congo.

Thirdly, the failure to construct a unified army was closely related to the problem of natural resources. The wars in Kivu had militarized the exploitation of resources and rerouted the parallel circuits of this exploitation to the capitals of neighbouring countries. In practice, many of the armed groups, if not all, integrated in the FARDC or not, survived economically because of their control over a mine, a trade route, a commercial centre or similar. And their leaders were not going to abandon this easily.

Finally, and perhaps most importantly, was a problem of a lack of transparency and poor governance. Enormous sums were circulating in the army. Tens of thousands of soldiers had to be paid, fed and transported, while ammunition and arms had to be purchased and dispatched. The army provided tremendous opportunities for its leaders to divert large sums. And the more unclear and shady the organization chart and the internal control mechanisms, without clear lines of command and accountability, the greater the opportunities for self-enrichment. Therefore, many people in key positions necessary for the unification of the army had a convincing financial argument to boycott it.

The aim was to reduce a mass of 165,000 registered combatants to a professional army of about 60,000 well-trained and disciplined soldiers. The problems were huge. A considerable number of the registered names were sick, elderly or dead soldiers. Then there were the fake names – people who had never existed but who now not only contributed to inflate the list and the alleged force of a militia, but enlarged the available budget as well. Samples provided indications that 25% to 30% of the names of registered military could never be deployed. The remaining 70% were officers or non-commissioned officers who thought they had an interest in remaining in the army, while a much larger proportion of the privates had left the army to reintegrate into civilian life. But most importantly, there were no appropriate mechanisms for vetting members of the new army for possible involvement in serious human rights abuses during the war.[32]

Congo had to form an army with people who had emerged from very different local realities, each with its own threats, balance of power, conflict potential and economic assets. Some of the officers had been trained in military school, others received their unofficial grades in the *maquis* of the war as part of rebel movements defending or attacking the nation. Many made an attempt to provide some stability and protection, but many others were notorious violators of human rights. All of them, though, grew up in a context where bad governance had sunk to the lowest levels.

Different partners in the international community had the ambition of helping the DRC transform its fluid landscape of militias into an instrument to enforce the rule of law. Individual countries such as France, Belgium, Angola and South Africa focused on the formation of individual brigades, and MONUSCO as well as the EU invested in security sector reforms. In 2005, the EU had created EUSEC to support and accompany the unification of the army, mainly by helping FARDC to carry out the biometric census of troops which reduced the possibility of claiming money for retired, dead or non-existent soldiers, and by separating the payment system and the command chain. These were significant steps forward but had important limitations. The impact of the technical contribution evaporated, not only because of the lack of ownership and commitment of the Congolese authorities, but also because EU staff were working from an artificial haven of relative peace, far away from the places where new (forced or voluntary) recruitments and desertions took place. Military operations were often chaotic and messed up administrative tools even before they were properly installed. The EUSEC tools were too static to make much difference in a dynamic conflict environment such as eastern Congo. As was the case in other programmes, the European approach focused too much on the technocratic accompaniment of formal exercises, while neglecting the political dimension, thus failing to ensure the credibility, quality and transparency of the process.

The result, then and now, is that a considerable part of the armed violence against the civilian population in Kivu is committed by the 'regular' army, which is supposed to protect it, by soldiers who recently left the army, or by people who are soldiers during the day and bandits at night. An inextricable entanglement of threads connects the Congolese army with the different armed groups in the east of the DRC.

The armed groups of foreign origin also remained an important source of violence against Congolese citizens. They had fought the regime in their own country but had been pushed back onto Congolese soil. The Ugandan Lord's Resistance Army (LRA) was one of the most violent rebel groups in the region, notorious for committing human rights violations including murder, mutilation, rape, widespread abductions of children and adults, sexual slavery and looting of villages. The LRA began in northern Uganda in 1987 as a result of the economic and political marginalization of the Acholi but degenerated into brutality against civilians, not only in Congo but also in the Central African Republic and South Sudan.

Another Ugandan armed group was ADF, the Alliance of Democratic Forces, which integrated the remnants of another rebel group, the National Army for the Liberation of Uganda (Nalu). The ADF was formed in the DRC in 1995 and located in the foothills of the Ruwenzori mountains at the DRC–Uganda border, launching its first attack against Uganda in 1996, but always remained one of the least known armed groups in the east of Congo. The rebellion periodically seemed to vanish and then reappear on the surface, creating the impression that it was more a constructed tool than a grassroots movement anchored in local realities. It has gradually received more attention throughout the years because of its alleged Islamic military agenda, with part of its leadership having converted to Islam. But it is difficult to find concrete and confirmed information on if and how ADF is connected to the larger networks of Islamic extremism.

The Burundian FNL remained active in the south of South Kivu. Congo had been very important in the struggle of Hutu rebels, and CNDD-FDD (*Conseil National Pour la Défense de la Démocratie – Forces pour la Défense de la Démocratie*) had been a major ally of Laurent Kabila during the Great War. But CNDD-FDD had laid down its arms in 2003 and won the elections in 2005. FNL was the last Burundian armed group still active, greatly weakened but with the capacity to be very destructive locally.

The LRA, ADF-Nalu and FNL were significant sources of local violence, but the most important and most threatening armed groups active in Congo after the 2006 elections were the FDLR and CNDP. The FDLR had been created (with Kabila senior's help) during the war to unite and deploy all pro-*ancien régime* Rwandan armed groups on Congolese soil against Rwanda and the RCD. The FDLR[33] emerged as the most powerful, organized and well-equipped rebel movement on the ground after the war, and put in place highly structured brigades in North and South Kivu. It has always been very difficult to determine the exact number of operational combatants at their disposal, because they lived in some form of symbiosis with the post-genocide exodus community of Hutu refugees in Congo, assessed at 245,000 according to a recent census conducted by the DRC National Commission for Refugees. Nearly 200,000 of them live in North Kivu and 42,000 in South Kivu. Many of them were born after the genocide and in Congo. The link with this community enabled the FDLR to mobilize and demobilize its militia members very fast. In 2007–2008, their operational force was estimated at 6,000.[34]

Eventually, many of the FDLR leaders who participated in the genocide left the movement or died, and it gradually absorbed a lot of the Congolese militia. In some places members of the FDLR settled down in local villages and intermingled with the community through marriage. But the FDLR has been responsible for extreme violence against Congolese citizens, including systematic rape and pillage. Much of this violence was strategic, aimed to give evidence of their nuisance capacity (and thus to be considered as a player to be taken into account), or to influence Congolese public opinion in periods when military operations were directed against them.

Relations between Congolese authorities and the FDLR have always been ambiguous, with the Congolese government reluctant to engage militarily against the FDLR. The DRC had actively supported the process of uniting into a new structure the remnants of the forces of the genocide on Congolese territory, Congolese officers had served under the FDLR, and the FDLR and FARDC had collaborated on several occasions in the past. At the same time, the DRC denied any political responsibility on the question of the FDLR, considering it a Rwandan problem, exported to Kivu by the international community.

Relations between the Rwandan authorities and the FDLR have been equally ambiguous. Over the years, the FDLR lost its capacity to deploy operations on Rwandan soil and its first-generation leadership largely disappeared, but the FDLR retained its genocidal image and continued to provoke strong reactions in Rwanda.[35] To become successful in its economic activities, though, it needed to commercialize the natural resources it exploited. Kigali had become the major hub of illicit trade, so to keep FDLR Ltd commercially viable, it had to establish a partnership with business circles in Kigali. That was possible through the Hutu soldiers who had been recruited by the Rwandan army, including former *génocidaires* (genocide perpetrators) who had been languishing in jail since 1994.[36]

The other major armed group, CNDP, was considered Congolese, and not a foreign-armed group. After the official withdrawal of the Rwandan troops in September 2002, Rwanda installed a series of mechanisms to control the economy in eastern Congo without the open presence of the Rwandan army. Rwandan businessmen replaced Congolese directors in charge of parastatal enterprises –

a number of soldiers stayed behind to continue to work in the mining sector, swapping their uniforms for suits. Through these demobilized soldiers, making use of Congolese Kinyarwanda-speakers who had become their agents, bribing unpaid local representatives of the Congolese state, Rwandan entrepreneurs continued to exploit the Kivu mines, employing local diggers and illegal landing strips. Different sources reported to the experts of the UN Panel that RCD officers, now formally part of the regular Congolese army but still loyal to Rwanda, used the security sector reforms and the integration of the army to bring Rwandan soldiers into both the FARDC and local defence forces.[37]

For a section of the Rwandan political and military elite, the CNDP was the main instrument to maintain its presence and a climate of impunity in Kivu. After his attempt to derail the transition by taking Bukavu in June 2004,[38] Nkunda kept a low profile for two years, while maintaining his armed group in some territories in both Masisi and Rutshuru. The fact that he was charged by the Congolese government with crimes against humanity obviously encouraged him to remain outside the army, and in December 2006 he launched the CNDP as an armed political movement, advancing a discourse of federalism, governance and cleaning up the mess of the Congolese state.

The fact that he claimed to defend the rights of the Tutsi as a community initially helped strengthen the coherence of the CNDP leadership, and reduced its capacity to recruit and mobilize. A lot of 'flotsam and jetsam from various tribes'[39] drifted towards the lower ranks of the CNDP, with MONUC demobilization programmes pushing many former militiamen into military unemployment, but even so the CNDP never managed to break outside of its self-imposed Tutsi label. Eventually it became dependent on fighters from Rwanda and forced recruitment.[40]

The relationship with Rwanda was ambiguous and delicate. The political elite in Kigali was gradually shifting towards a development model that would make it the Singapore of Africa with a glossy plan called Vision 2020, which was difficult to reconcile with an image coloured by warlords, plundering and mass rape. But not everybody in Rwanda shared that vision and of course the material stakes remained very high. The December 2008 report of the Expert Panel of the United Nations described in great detail how this rebellion received support from commercial networks in Rwanda, and from individuals in highly strategic positions within the Rwandan political and military authorities.

It is not easy to have an accurate idea of the number of combatants the CNDP deployed. Around 2005–2006 the rebellion seemed too small to do much harm, so small in fact that the government effectively wallowed in complacency after its electoral victory and lost focus. As Prunier put it: 'For the past two years the Congolese government has looked like a beached whale, incapable of moving in spite of its bulk. This created an opportunity which Nkunda has exploited'.[41] So Nkunda grew. Maybe he did not become the large Congolese movement he wanted, but he recruited young Tutsi both in the DRC and in neighbouring countries, including demobilized soldiers and the unemployed. Eventually he commanded an army of 6,000 to 9,000 combatants, much fewer than the FARDC, but they were more motivated, better trained and more disciplined than their adversaries.[42]

After a relatively calm period, Nkunda once again opened Pandora's box. In May 2007, the FDLR killed the entire population of Kanyola in South Kivu, accusing the villagers of supporting the CNDP,[43] and in response at least a dozen other armed groups in Kivu swung back into action. Hunde, Tembo, Nyanga, Nande and Hutu communities felt insecure facing CNDP and unprotected by the FARDC, so they organized to defend themselves.[44]

The military polarization between the Congolese national army and Nkunda's CNDP in the final months of 2007 created an extremely explosive situation, not only for the democratic process in the DRC, but also in terms of risking a renewed full-scale war in the region. An immediate consequence of the fighting was a large increase in the number of Congolese refugees and internally displaced persons (IDPs). After negotiations in 2007, an attempt was made to form six mixed brigades with CNDP rebels and soldiers of the 'regular' army, but the idea didn't last long. The agreement fell apart before the end of the year and Kinshasa launched a large-scale offensive against Nkunda, resulting in a humiliating defeat for government forces.[45]

The Congolese government organized a conference on peace, security and development in the provinces of North and South Kivu from 6 to 24 January 2008. The conference was backed by the international community and co-chaired by the speaker of Parliament Vital Kamerhe (a Shi from Walungu) and the president of the electoral commission Abbé Malumalu (a Nande from Butembo). The ambition was to involve the communities and address the root causes of the conflict. In spite of various weaknesses – in particular the haste and lack of preparation of the proceedings, and a certain ambiguity in their terms of reference – the conference had an important outcome with the signing on 23 January of the 'Acte de l'engagement pour la paix' (Act of Engagement for Peace) by the various armed protagonists, including the Congolese government and twenty-two armed groups. Alongside the Nairobi Accord signed on 9 November 2007 between Rwanda and Congo, the Act, if respected and fully implemented, constituted a historic moment to consolidate peace.

But, of course, it didn't. Both the government and the CNDP continued to prepare for more fighting. The government concentrated 20,000 soldiers around Goma who proved incapable of preventing the CNDP from taking the city in October 2008. Eventually, though, the rebels did not move into Goma, not because the town was successfully defended by the army or the UN peacekeeping troops, but because when Nkunda was about to enter the city he received a phone call from Kigali telling him not to do so.

This was an important moment which made clear that there was never such a thing as a unified Rwandan or Tutsi agenda for Congo.

Not only have there always been divisions between the Congolese Tutsi community and the Rwandan political elite, which was Tutsi as well; as we shall see in the following chapters there were serious internal divisions as to how to deal with Kivu.

Chapter 4

UMOJA WETU AND KAGAME'S BRAVE NEW WORLD

In 2007 and 2008 the shadow of Laurent Nkunda was hanging heavily over eastern Congo. He was in a position to become a real phenomenon, because his rebel movement was being supported by the political elite of RCD/Goma for whom the 2006 elections had been a landslide defeat. They had held significant posts during the transition, but the polls had swept them away and they no longer felt represented by the institutions of the Third Republic. Nkunda also received support from private business circles of mainly Tutsi entrepreneurs, from both Rwanda and Congo.[1] The presence of the CNDP allowed them to sustain the economic impunity they needed to continue the illicit exploitation of Congo's natural resources. Nkunda received support from people inside the Rwandan government and army who provided logistical (medical supplies, food, ammunition) and even direct military support for important military operations. Taxing the local population in some parts of Rutshuru and Masisi and control of the border post of Bunagana also allowed Nkunda to establish economic independence. All this had been extensively documented by the report of the UN Group of Experts[2] released in December 2008. But the main reason Nkunda's influence was able to grow was the mismanagement of security sector reform.

All of a sudden, in August 2008, Nkunda fell silent. He disappeared entirely from the radar, and people in the diplomatic services and in the press started to speculate about his health and whether he was in fact dead. In October he resurfaced with a new style and a new plan. He took time to meet the press and international diplomats, receiving delegations in a classic light suit, white shirt and a red tie, toying with a black walking stick with a silver handle. The discourse changed as well. Instead of talking about defending the Tutsi community against the FDLR, his purported mission now was to fight bad governance, review the Chinese contracts and promote national reconciliation. Interviewed by David Van Reybrouck,[3] he called himself the Congolese Charles de Gaulle. In this period, he intensified contacts with other forces of the Congolese opposition and developed a charismatic, almost visionary appearance, speech and body language, using the press to present a more intellectual image to the world instead of as the warlord who was responsible for massacres in Kisangani in 2002, Bukavu in 2004 or North Kivu since 2006. In short, Nkunda tried to present himself as an autonomous political force, no longer an RCD/Goma B-plan or proxy of Rwanda. Three months later, he was arrested in a joint operation by the Congolese and Rwandan army and placed under house arrest.

The joint operation between the Rwandan army (RDF) and Congo (FARDC) was deployed on 20 January 2009, the day the entire world was glued to the television screen to watch Barack Obama being inaugurated as president of the United States. The joint operation was named '*Umoja Wetu*' (Swahili for 'Our Unity') and the objective was twofold: to dismantle the FDLR in North Kivu and to end the CNDP rebellion by integrating its combatants into the FARDC. The operation was the result of a secret negotiation process between Kagame and Kabila in the final months of 2008, where both parties agreed that Nkunda should be dismissed and the FDLR disarmed. For Kabila, Nkunda had become a source of perpetual humiliation for him in Congolese and international public opinion. For Kagame, Nkunda had always been problematic because the Congolese issues profoundly divided his political elite. Rwanda's presence in Congo had been used by certain generals to

create an economic and political power base which was kept outside
Kagame's direct control, and Kigali had been criticized for its DRC
policies, even by its loyal partners. But since Nkunda had given up
the defence of the Tutsi as his primary mission in order to position
himself as a Congolese leader, with a Congolese political agenda,
he had lost Kagame's confidence entirely. The operations were
commanded jointly by the Rwandan chief of staff James Kabarebe
and the inspector-general of the Congolese police John Numbi.[4] The
supreme command of the FARDC (led by General Didier Etumba)
remained entirely outside the planning process and operations.[5]
The political architect on the Congolese side had been Kabila's
advisor Augustin Katumba Mwanke. Neither the government nor
Parliament had been informed of what was being prepared, with
the speaker of Parliament Vital Kamerhe protesting that he had not
been told in advance and calling it unconstitutional. Kabila considered Kamerhe's public criticism disloyal at such a delicate moment,
and the debate escalated quickly, ending with the departure of Vital
Kamerhe as speaker of Parliament on 26 March 2009.

On 22 January 2009, two days after the beginning of *Umoja
Wetu*, Laurent Nkunda was arrested on Rwandan soil, very much
to his surprise. The arrest was made public in a statement signed by
John Numbi as chief of staff of the joint operation. The purpose was
to extradite Nkunda in the following days to Kinshasa, but when
this rumour spread in the field, it caused great animosity among the
CNDP officers, in refugee camps for Congolese Tutsi on Rwandan
soil and inside the Rwandan army. After all, he had served as an
RPF rebel and remained extremely well connected in the army. The
extradition was cancelled and Nkunda remained under house arrest
in Rwanda with an unclear legal status, since there were no charges
against him in Rwanda.

Concretely, the joint operation was mainly conducted by the
Rwandan army and the CNDP under a FARDC label. John Numbi
was the chief of staff, but the rest of the FARDC was largely absent.
MONUC did not participate in *Umoja Wetu*. The UN Mission was

not at all involved in the first part of the operations, and in later campaigns its support was mainly logistical, but this did not give MONUC the status of a partner of the operations or the possibility of having any impact on them. The Congo authorities kept MONUC at sufficient distance to exclude it from the planning and carrying out of the operation but at times close enough to give it responsibility in case of failure or loss of control. The ambiguity of this position provoked discussion about the different aspects of MONUC's mandate – on one side protection of the civilian population and on the other partnership with the FARDC at a time when it had become a danger to the civilian population. The joint operation did not share any information with the UN Mission.

Laurent Nkunda was replaced as leader of the CNDP by his deputy Bosco Ntaganda, nicknamed 'the Terminator'. Ntaganda was born on the Rwandan–Congolese border in 1973, and had joined the Rwandan Patriotic Front in its struggle against Habyarimana. His first documented atrocities were committed when he fought between 2002 and 2005 in Ituri, as a commander of Thomas Lubanga's *Union des Patriotes Congolais* (UPC). The ICC had issued its first sealed arrest warrant against Ntaganda in 2006, but he evaded justice and joined the CNDP. Ntaganda was accused by the ICC of war crimes and five counts of crimes against humanity, for murder and attempted murder, attacks against civilians, rape and sexual slavery, the recruitment and use of child soldiers and pillaging in 2002 and 2003.[6]

Ntaganda's nomination as leader of the CNDP made him a commanding officer in the Congolese army and deputy chief of staff of *Umoja Wetu*, with his first and foremost mission being to integrate the CNDP into the army. International public opinion was outraged. Because of the ICC arrest warrant against him, diplomats in Goma refused to meet him or attend gatherings in which Ntaganda participated. Congolese government circles found that hypocritical: how could they avoid Bosco but happily shake hands with somebody such as General Gabriel Amisi, nicknamed Tango

Four, who had held much more senior positions in the RCD-Goma and overseen many more atrocities than Bosco? He had joined the FARDC during the transition and his reputation was whitewashed. International and Congolese civil society, though, considered Ntaganda's nomination as a posthumous insult to every Congolese who had died because of the war.

For Congo and Rwanda, *Umoja Wetu* was not a passionate romance but rather a marriage of convenience. The joint operation existed because the two countries had few other options. Joseph Kabila, powerless with his phantom army facing the CNDP backed by Rwanda, had requested military help. The African Union, the Southern African Development Community, the European Union and individual countries such as Angola had considered sending troops but, at the end of the day, nobody came to his aid.

Rwanda for its part had had a difficult few months. In addition to the problems created by the international arrest warrants issued by the Spanish judge Fernando Andreu Merelles and the French judge Jean Louis Bruguière against top officials of the RPF,[7] Rwanda was engaged in a painful argument with the EU over the publication of the observation report on the September 2008 legislative elections.[8] In December of the same year the UN experts' report was published, with plenty of detail on Rwandan support for Laurent Nkunda. Sweden and the Netherlands immediately suspended part of their budgetary aid, while in the British press there were clear demands that the UK's unconditional support should stop. Kabila had no other option than to participate in *Umoja Wetu* because he had been left alone in the face of a humiliating political and military situation. Kagame had no other option because he was confronted with a changed attitude on the part of partners who had formerly supported him.

Later in 2009 *Umoja Wetu* was followed up by other campaigns: *Amani Leo* ('Peace Today' in Swahili) and *Kimya II* ('Tranquillity' in Lingala). A year after the launch of the military operations it was clear that their stated objectives had not been attained. The

CNDP was certainly decapitated by the arrest of Laurent Nkunda but proper integration into the Congolese state had not happened. Part of the CNDP was never integrated into the army and for the part that was, the question was: 'Who finally integrated whom?' Military integration of forces that were formerly enemies is a long and difficult process even under optimum conditions. The 'integration' of the CNDP into the FARDC at the start of Umoja Wetu, however, was undertaken very quickly with very little outside help and in the middle of a military operation. The present-day result of the integration of the CNDP is that it is larger than before and controls more troops and a considerably greater geographical area. The CNDP's chain of command has remained intact and since the movement is now part of the 'regular' army this has become a parallel chain of command. In many parts of Kivu the CNDP's parallel administration, including roadblocks, remains in place. Most of all, as a result of Umoja Wetu and Kimia II, CNDP units have gained access to economically desirable places. Financially it was dependent on what it was given by various Rwandan sources, by the business community in Goma and by controlling imports and exports at the Bunagana frontier post. Deployment as part of the military operations has given it a hold on one of the most lucrative mineral areas in both Kivus.

The Umoja Wetu campaign had changed the CNDP leadership radically. Laurent Nkunda was replaced on the initiative of Rwanda by Bosco Ntaganda, who came from a different geographical background (Masisi not Rutshuru) and a different clan (Gogwe not Jomba). Bosco is not an intellectual, nor is he charismatic. He joined the CNDP relatively late and is wanted by the ICC. This change of leadership has revealed major divisions in the CNDP. It has split into several factions, which on several occasions have been on the verge of fighting each other. Similarly in its civil structure new men have come and gone. Thus the CNDP has been weakened by disunity. While at first sight the CNDP appears the winner of the integration process, consolidating its hold on the east and preparing for its reign, this is not in reality true. The CNDP does not really exist as an organization and this has contributed to increasing chaos, disorder and impunity in the region.

As far as the FDLR was concerned, the military operations resolved nothing. When *Umoja Wetu* was deployed, FDLR units avoided direct confrontation and withdrew from their positions. Where possible, they took them back, avenging themselves on Congolese civilians much more violently than they had in previous years. I was in North Kivu at the time and was shown a letter written by the FDLR commander ordering his brigades to carry out violent actions against villagers and commit massacres in order to provoke a fierce public reaction against *Umoja Wetu*, thus forcing negotiations.[9] Not every brigade obeyed. In North Kivu, the FDLR had always carried out a rotation of its forces, which meant that no ties had been established with local communities. The links with the Congolese population were more developed in South Kivu. *Umoja Wetu* dispersed their units but failed to dismantle their chain of command or neutralize their operational forces. FDLR combatants were wounded, died or surrendered, but other people were recruited, or joined after leaving the FARDC or other armed groups.

For the FARDC, the operations were very confusing: the units fighting side by side with the Rwandan army were the recently integrated CNDP brigades, now wearing FARDC uniforms. *Umoja Wetu* soon became a parallel structure, an army within the army. There was also evidence that not only Congolese Tutsi had integrated into the army from the CNDP, but also a number of Rwandan soldiers, though it is difficult to prove exact numbers.

Instead of talking about *Umoja Wetu* (Our Unity) and *Amani Leo* (Peace Today), the population nicknamed the operations *Umoja Gani?* ('Which Unity?' in Swahili) and *Amani Wapi?* ('Where is the Peace?' in Swahili).

For the average FARDC soldier without a CNDP background, the operations were bewildering: it was difficult to understand who, after all, were friends and who were enemies. For years they had been involved in fierce fighting against the CNDP, but now they were supposed to become comrades and the CNDP's leaders were taking command. Many soldiers from Kivu refused to leave their region to be deployed elsewhere under the FARDC, because they knew they would be living in extremely poor conditions, without the slightest idea when they would be able to return home and re-join the families they had left behind in an unstable and insecure environment. A lot of them simply ran away and were recruited by the armed groups, including the FDLR.

Kagame's brave new world in motion

The interaction between Congo and Rwanda has had a significant impact on both countries, through connected identity issues, overlapping conflicts and trans-border economic interests. After the official end of the war in 2002, Rwanda's shadow continued to weigh heavily on Congo and its eastern provinces. But Congo influenced Rwanda too. The RPF rebuilt and reorganized the country at an unlikely speed after the genocide. A new Rwanda was shaped but the regime was not static at all, with internal dynamics and changing attitudes among its most loyal partners putting it under pressure. Congo was an important issue in these processes.

In October 1990, the Rwandan Patriotic Front, founded in the Tutsi refugee camps in Uganda, invaded Rwanda in an attempt to reconquer the country their fathers had been forced to leave in previous waves of violence. Their historical leader Fred Rwigyema was killed on the third day of the struggle and replaced by Paul Kagame, who led the RPF to victory in July 1994. He became vice-president and minister of defence in the transitional government installed after the Rwandan genocide. In March 2000, President Pasteur Bizimungu resigned in a dispute over the make-up of a new cabinet, to be replaced by Kagame.

Over the years, the RPF has built up its control over public life (including the political and judicial organs) along the lines of a one-party system. This has happened despite the existence of a number of satellite political parties operating on the fringes of power which, however, do not seriously dispute their basic loyalty to that power. The presidential election of 2003, which brought the country's political transition to an end, was organized without any real political space: the only true opposition party did not receive official approval, and the main independent candidates for the presidential elections were disqualified on the eve of polling day. The campaign was accompanied by disappearances, arrests and intimidation of candidates, the electorate and observers. President Kagame won the election with 95% of the vote.

The European Union reported irregularities and serious fraud in both the legislative and presidential elections of 2003. The EU observation mission had similar findings during the legislative elections of September 2008. Although the wording of the report and in the declarations made at the time of its publication was very diplomatic and tried to avoid confrontation with the Rwandan regime, several of those who took part in this mission reported irregularities in the handling of ballot boxes and in counting votes.

In the election of 2010, Kagame faced three candidates who were considered by the traditional opposition as 'satellite candidates, phoney opposition players intended to maintain the illusion of pluralism'.[10] The months before the elections had been very tense, with the more genuine opposition parties starting to prepare their campaigns: the Social Party Imberakuri (PSI) led by Bernard Ntaganda; the Green Democratic Party (GDP) with a leadership that came mainly from the Anglophone community and which, according to many, was a result of the discontent within the RPF; and lastly the Unified Democratic Forces (UDF-Inkingi), formed around presidential candidate Victoire Ingabire, who had returned to Rwanda in January after an absence of seventeen years. The leaders of these parties confronted hostility and significant verbal aggression from the authorities and media. Victoire Ingabire in particular, with her clear message and direct, flamboyant style received a lot of national and international attention. However, when the election actually arrived, none of these candidates was able to formally run for office. Eventually, Kagame was re-elected on 9 August 2010 with an overwhelming 93% of the vote.

But in March 2010, four months before the election, a major crack appeared on the surface of the ruling elite. General Faustin Kayumba Nyamwasa, a long-time companion of President Kagame and former commander in chief of the Rwandan army, left Rwanda and its regime to join the dissident Colonel Patrick Karegeya, a former intelligence chief who lived in exile in Johannesburg. In the months after Nyamwasa's departure, others left too – influential and high-profile people like Theodore Rudasingwa (Kagame's former *chef de cabinet*), Gerald Gahima (former prosecutor-general and vice-president of the Supreme Court) and Kagame's private secretary David Himbara. All of a sudden, Kagame was not struggling with his traditional enemies but with his frustrated comrades-in-arms. The ruling inner circle was losing its coherence and had to fight against its own disintegration. When it looked at itself, it was confronted with the cracks in the mirror that belied the united image it wanted to show the public in Rwanda as well as internationally.

President Kagame accused Karegeya and Kayumba of attempting to destabilize Rwanda. Kagame had been at odds with both officers for several years. Faustin Kayumba Nyamwasa grew up in the south of Uganda and became one of the most powerful people in the Rwandan army, leading the military campaigns in the northeast of the country in the years following the genocide. In 2001 he was replaced as head of the army and sent for training to the United Kingdom. In 2004, he was appointed ambassador to India. Political insiders in Rwanda have always believed that this appointment was a step taken by President Kagame to remove Kayumba from the centre of politico-military affairs in Rwanda as he was starting to build his own base within the inner circle of power in Rwanda. Patrick Karegeya was not only the former intelligence chief, he was also in charge of the Congo Desk, a bureau run by the External

Security Department which was created in order to manage the exploitation of the wealth of eastern DRC, the income from which did not appear in official government accounts. This system enabled the army and political leaders to conceal huge sums of money. In all the discussions and documents relating to the official withdrawal of the Rwandan army from the Congo in September 2002 it has been very hard to distinguish precisely between the role of the Rwandan state and that of the non-state political and military lobbies regarding the illicit exploitation of Congolese resources and the support given to military groups such as the CNDP. The shadowy zone between the official institutions and the informal lobbies and interest groups effectively acted as a state within the state. Patrick Karegeya occupied the central position in that space.

In several interviews after his departure in the Ugandan and South African press, General Kayumba spoke of the transformation of Kagame's regime into a dictatorship and of his own commitment to a democratic Rwanda. It has always been difficult and not very useful to try to draw a line between hawks and doves within the Rwandan political and military elite. Even so, under no circumstances were Kayumba and Karegeya to be considered doves.

There were many bones of contention dividing the RPF's top echelon. Legal procedures initiated in France and in Spain had badly shaken the heads of the army and government in Kigali. In November 2006, the French judge Jean-Louis Bruguière had issued an international arrest warrant against Kayumba and eight other high-ranking military men close to Kagame in connection with the enquiry into the attack on President Habyarimana's aeroplane on 6 April 1994, which triggered the genocide. In February 2008, the Spanish magistrate Andreu Merelles issued forty arrest warrants against senior officers in the Rwanda army (including Kayumba) for acts of genocide, crimes against humanity, war crimes and terrorism committed in Rwanda and in the DRC between 1 October 1990 and 2002. The cases had been submitted to the Spanish courts in 2000 by relatives of Spanish victims killed in Rwanda, religious and humanitarian workers and by exiled Rwandan organizations. The Rwandan government could rely on the loyalty of a number of countries and international institutions, and this was at least partly based on feelings of guilt at not having been able to prevent the genocide and, frankly, not having tried to do so. To preserve international support, it was vital for the Rwandan regime to be sure of the global interpretation of Rwanda's recent history. Since 1994, the country had been ruled in a climate of winners of the war versus its losers, the victims of the crimes against their executioners. An entirely new juridical system had been put in place through the *gacaca*[11] courts to deal with crimes of genocide against Tutsis while at the same time there has been a complete taboo regarding crimes committed by the RPF since the start of the war. This taboo reduced the potentially positive effects that the *gacaca* should have been able to have: instead of being the means of taking on board the traumatic past, the *gacaca* have become a strategy for consolidating the winners/ victims versus losers/criminals scenario.[12]

So Bruguière and Andreu Merelles' initiatives were exasperating for the Rwandan regime, disrupting the image they wished to protect. Even though it was highly unlikely that the current leaders of Rwanda would be brought to trial in France or Spain, sooner or later the question would have to be: 'What are we going to admit? Who shall we sacrifice?' Such questions did not help to create internal cohesion. Kayumba's departure was a major concern for the regime. What would he say and before which audience? What if he was extradited to Spain? Hence the pressure on the South African government to send him back to Rwanda.

Since 1996 the Congo has taken up a lot of space in Rwanda's foreign policy. On several occasions what has happened in the Congo has been a source of discord within the regime. Kayumba, for instance, was heavily opposed to the confrontations with Uganda in 2000 and 2002. The arrest of Laurent Nkunda provoked much animosity in Rwanda, not only in Congolese Rwandophone refugee circles and camps in Rwanda, but also in the army. After all, Nkunda had served in the RPF and elements of the RPF had served in Nkunda's forces. This collaboration created strong links and common interests. Directly linked to the Rwandan involvement in Congo is the problem of demobilized soldiers. Now that a direct presence in the Congo is no longer an option, Rwanda finds itself with much too large an army. Part of the surplus can be deployed by the African Union, but that is a limited option. The remainder has to be demobilized, and many of these ex-soldiers feel abandoned by a regime they have fought for, often in very tough circumstances. Also divisive for the Rwandan elite is the wealth extracted from the eastern provinces of Congo; a good part is outside the control of the Rwandan government even though it serves the interests of key people in the Rwandan political–military establishment. Thus, the tension existing between Karegeya and Kagame was not about democracy in Rwanda and peace in the region. In the first place it was about Karegeya resisting Kagame's efforts to dismantle the parallel economic structure, the almost state within a state Karegeya had created with the Congo Desk, and the new regulations that meant Rwandan leaders had to report their wealth and income transparently.[13]

Some Rwandan analysts do point out that membership of clans is an important aspect of the identity of a number of those currently active on the political stage. But the significance of these Tutsi clans, at least as far as Rwanda is concerned, lies mostly in the past rather than in the present. The kinship element is minimal now and these cleavages are used to reinforce and justify other issues, such as regional or political differences, and are probably not the causes of conflict as such. In the Congolese Tutsi community, clan divisions play a much more active role in the present, and this will be returned to later. Furthermore, language remained a factor of division in the country. Rwanda had been a UN trust territory under Belgian administration and had adopted French as the national language after independence. The post-colonial regime was defeated by a rebel movement, and was born and bred in Rwandan refugee camps in Uganda. The new leaders had grown up speaking English and in 2008 English was recognized as the official language in education. For some this was a visionary decision to open up the country to the regional, continental and global reality, but for others it was a decision to set in stone the ambition of a minority regime to monopolize communication and the country's intellectual life, to dominate the country's youth, to rewrite history and in the end to take control of the country's collective memory. Kayumba Nyamwasa's departure caused a lot of unrest, not only in the Rwandan army but also in eastern Congo. There were many indications that Nyamwasa and Karegeya were investigating if it was possible to organize an armed resistance on Congolese soil, bringing together people from backgrounds as diverse as the part of the CNDP that had stayed loyal to Nkunda, certain Mai Mai groups, the FRF (*Forces Républicaines Fédéralistes*) rebels from the Banyamulenge community in the south of South Kivu, bits of the FARDC and the FNL. Contacts were even made with some commanders within the FDLR. All these forces had their reasons to oppose Kagame and the ambition was to unite them in an ad hoc movement against the regime in Kigali. To do that, they had to reconcile water and fire. I travelled extensively in Kivu at that time and talked to people in most of the groups, my conclusion being that they had tried but failed. A member of the Rwandan opposition in London and self-declared supporter of Kayumba Nyamwasa even asked me if I could facilitate communication with certain DRC Mai Mai leaders – something I did not do.

One of the reasons for this failure was that Kayumba Nyamwasa simply did not have the profile or the temperament to reconcile water and fire, and was considered a hardliner of Kagame's regime. He was not perceived as a likely alternative who could be a motor for change.

Three weeks after Kagame's re-election, the French newspaper *Le Monde* leaked the draft of the UN's DRC Mapping Exercise Report, which aimed to document the most serious violations of human rights in the DRC between March 1993 and June 2003. In paragraph 517, the report states:

The systematic and widespread attacks described in this report, which targeted very large numbers of Rwandan Hutu refugees and members of the Hutu civilian population, resulting in their death, reveal a number of damning elements that, if they were proven before a competent court, could be classified as crimes of genocide.[14]

This was like an earthquake for Rwanda, more so even than the international juridical procedures of Bruguière and Andreu Merelles. For a decade and a half the regime embodied the victory of genocide victims over those who had perpetrated it. The report, published on 1 October 2010, suggested that this might only be one side of the story; that the reality of Rwanda's traumatic recent history might be much more complex.

The report was a very extensive inventory of the most important human rights violations in one decade, and as such was not a basis for prosecution. Most of the facts reported by the UN researchers were known, but for the first time they were brought together and acknowledged at the level of an official UN document. Two and a half years after the UN Office of the High Commissioner for Human Rights published the report, there had been insufficient follow-up by the governments in Africa's Great Lakes region and by the UN itself. The mapping report caused problems for Kagame and his entourage, but it helped to solve its most important problem of that moment. The report created so much pressure on the regime and the Tutsi community that it encouraged them to close ranks. The exodus of party members and army officers to join the dissidents stopped. By the end of 2010 it became clear that Kayumba Nyamwasa would not be able to raise international support for an armed initiative.

2010 had been an *annus horribilis* for Paul Kagame, with Ingabire's return, Kayumba Nyawasa's dissidence and the international impact of the mapping report. But he had managed to organize his re-election and knew no new major challenges were to be expected from inside the country. Kayumba's failure to set up a larger coalition at the end of the year was another reassurance for Kagame. His firm control over Rwanda and the alliance with Kabila since *Umoja Wetu* placed him in a comfortable position for 2011.

Chapter 5

THE 2011 ELECTION

An election following historic elections is often problematic. The electoral process in the Congo had led to the setting up of its first legitimate institutions, even if there was a long delay in their actually being implemented. Below the provincial level, the elections had never even been properly organized, which gave Congo's democratic architecture something of a heavy roof, weak walls and no proper foundations. Throughout the term of office following 2006, the integration of armed forces remained a priority for the government and for partners in the Congo, but on the ground there had not been much real progress. The second electoral cycle was expected to be very complicated. Kabila was in a much stronger position as an elected president seeking to renew his mandate, and the international community would be much less involved than five years earlier. The process would attract far less attention from the international media and observers.

It was predictable that, after the Congolese elections in 2006, the political system would develop a tension between the semi-presidential system as defined by the constitution and the apparent wish of the head of state, legitimized by the elections, to install a presidential regime.[1] The impact of the government remained limited, but with Vital Kamerhe as its speaker, the National Assembly had grown in its role. The Parliament had claimed and conquered its own space as the legislature before which the government was accountable. But of course a lot of decisions were taken and carried out by the parallel circuit led by Kabila.

With Kamerhe's departure as speaker of Parliament, the democratic deficit increased, as well as the number of cases of intimidation, arbitrary arrests and other violations of human rights against journalists, leaders of civil society and the opposition.[2]

Almost halfway between two elections, Kamerhe's exit also marked the start of election fever. Several Congolese insiders told me there was a silent agreement between Kabila and Kamerhe, whereby Kamerhe would support Kabila's re-election in 2011, and in return Kabila would support Kamerhe as his successor in 2016. But the visibility and popularity that Kamerhe had gained as speaker was considered extremely worrying by at least part of Kabila's entourage, including Katumba Mwanke and Evariste Boshab,[3] who had other scenarios in mind for the post-2016 era. Many people read the polarization against Kamerhe as orchestrated by Katumba Mwanke and Boshab, with the latter eventually succeeding Kamerhe as speaker of Parliament.

The political move against Kamerhe was an important development in the inner circle of the regime. Katumba Mwanke had taken much more of a leading role after the elections. Without Kamerhe, the Katangese influence in the presidential space was reinforced. The regime's top priority was to ensure its re-election in 2011 and guarantee its survival in power in the long run. It was obvious that the strategic decisions would be taken by a very small group of people whose relative cohesion was based on common interests but even so there were potential cleavages between them. From 2008 onwards, it became increasingly clear that the traditional antagonism between North and South Katanga also divided Kabila's inner circle, as embodied in Katumba Mwanke (South) and John Numbi (North), with the potential for not only the regime but also the state to implode.

Katanga is a complex province, rich in minerals and more industrialized than the rest of the country. However, Katanga does not exhibit development indicators above the national average, largely because there are enormous discrepancies between its territories and districts. Kabila is via his father a member of the Balubakat community – the Baluba from North Katanga. Both Kabila regimes (*père* and *fils*) are perceived in Congo as Swahili-speaking Katanga-based strongholds. The north of the province, where the Balubakat originate, has been largely absent in the growth dynamics observable in the major cities, such as Lubumbashi, Likasi and Kolwezi, a rich mining region which supplies cobalt, copper, tin, radium, uranium and diamonds.

An important milestone for Congo was the celebration of the fiftieth anniversary of independence, on 30 June 2010. Kabila considered it not only the solemn commemoration of half a century of sovereignty, but also a prestige project to show an embellished more attractive and modern capital to the world, and an opportunity to win back some of the popularity he had lost because the concrete achievements of the first legislature of the Third Republic had fallen well below the expectations of the people. The renovation and improvement of some of the main roads, squares and intersections in town eased the traffic situation and some statues were erected.

The public relations dimension of the celebration was severely damaged when, on 2 June, the human rights activist Floribert Chebeya was found murdered in a car at the side of the road in one of the suburbs of Kinshasa. There were obvious signs of serious assault, but without a clearly ascertainable cause of death. Various pieces of evidence were found in the car to make it look like a sex crime or a crime of passion. His driver, Fidèle Bazana, was reported missing. Chebeya, president of *La Voix des Sans-Voix* (The Voice of the Voiceless), had been a pioneer of the human rights movement since the era of Mobutu. On the day of his death, he had an appointment with the chief of the national police John Numbi concerning the inhumane treatment of prisoners in Congo. All aspects of the investigation led to Numbi and half a week later his supporters inside the army and the presidential guard were neutralized, and the man himself suspended. Numbi – another key figure in Kabila's inner circle – vanished for a long time into the wings, though he was never tried. A military court in 2011 convicted the deputy chief of police special services, Colonel Daniel Mukalay, of murder and sentenced him to death, together with three other officers. A fifth policeman was jailed for life, but three of the convicted policemen are still on the run.[4]

The assassination of Chebeya shook the world. Several countries threatened to suspend their participation in the festivities, but in the end twenty-six countries sent delegations. Although Congolese and international public opinion was shocked by Chebeya's death, nobody went as far as to boycot the ceremony. The Belgian King Albert II was the guest of honour, the first monarch of the former colonizer to visit the country in twenty-five years. Robert Mugabe, Paul Kagame, Yoweri Museveni and Ali Bongo, presidents of Zimbabwe, Rwanda, Uganda and Gabon respectively, participated, as well as many other prominent guests.

After the fiftieth anniversary celebrations, the Congolese government remained in campaign mode and sped up the electoral process, hoping to capitalize on the visibility it obtained around the *Cinquantenaire*. The regime was confident that it would control the process, aware of its unpopularity but knowing that it had no opponents of any stature. This changed in December 2010. Etienne Tshisekedi returned to the country after years of absence to announce his participation in the presidential elections. Two weeks later, Kamerhe left the PPRD, joined an opposition party, UNC (*Union pour la Nation Congolaise*), and declared he would run a campaign against Kabila in the presidential elections as well. Both the UDPS and the UNC had succeeded in mobilizing many people for their candidates and it looked as if Congo was moving towards an electoral battle between protagonists with different visions and models for society.

The constitutional revision of January 2011 changed things again, taking both Congolese and international actors and observers by surprise. It was carried out in a very short time when diplomats were just (or not yet) returning from their holidays and when the world's attention was focused on the referendum in South Sudan and on the post-electoral situation in Côte d'Ivoire. The main consequence of the revision was that the presidential elections would be organized in a single round. The importance of this cannot be over-emphasized. It prevented the political parties from using the first round as a trial run to test the electoral power balance amongst them and to allow a final challenger to gather broader support in the second round. Kabila's bet was that it was unlikely he would be beaten if he faced all his adversaries in only one round, unless they managed to coalesce their campaign around a single candidate of a united opposition. He considered the opposition too divided, and the leaders too preoccupied with their own egos, to set up an efficient alliance and a joint candidate. The constitutional revision also set the tone for the leverage the international community could have on forthcoming events: it would be very difficult to find the proper space and content for any critical messages it may wish to send in the course of the electoral process, not having reacted to the constitutional revision in the first place.

Many issues and concerns marked the preparation for the elections, for instance in regard to the electoral commission. Apollinaire Malumalu had chaired the electoral commission organizing the historic elections of 2006. After that, he got involved in the negotiations with the armed groups in the east, acting as co-chair of the Goma Conference in January 2008 and coordinating the large development programmes set up following the conference. He remained president of the commission, although his involvement in the implementation of Kabila's plans in eastern Congo affected his credibility as an independent civil society leader representing the churches.

In February 2011 the president set up a new electoral commission. Its name changed from CEI to CENI, the Independent National Electoral Commission, and Kabila appointed as chair Daniel Mulunda Ngoy, a pastor of the New Methodist Church with a master's degree in peace and conflict resolution studies. Of course two questions remained: did Mulunda Ngoy have the technical skills and capacities to organize free and fair elections before the president's first mandate expired according to the constitution, and would he – as a member of Kabila's Balubakat community and the president's religious advisor – have enough strength of personality and political will to act as an autonomous force who could guarantee the genuine independence of the commission?

The months before the elections were tense. The assassination of Chebeya had been foreshadowed by the repressive grip the regime imposed on its citizens to ensure its re-election. UN investigators reported 188 cases of human rights violations before the official campaign began in October. Violence perpetrated by police and other state security services included restrictions on political activities, unnecessary force against demonstrators and arbitrary arrests primarily directed toward opposition parties, their supporters and journalists.[5]

It is difficult to make predictions in a country without serious polls. Many people had the strong feeling that there was a hard-to-quantify anti-Kabila sentiment among the population, but the opposition had to work in very difficult circumstances. The opposition parties knew they had to present a joint candidate if they wanted to beat Kabila, but this turned out to be as difficult as expected. Until the very last moment, there were talks among the various main leaders (Etienne Tshisekedi of the UDPS, Vital Kamerhe of the UNC, Kengo wa Dondo of the MLC), but in various phases of the negotiations Tshisekedi's non-inclusive approach stood in the way of a broad political platform which could have been a challenge to Kabila.

The opposition parties were institutionally fragile, strategically weak and/or internally divided. In many cases parties were created around the personality of their historical leader or his heirs. Due to this personalization of structures, an opposition party is often seen as representing a particular region of the country or a specific group in the population. Even though the UDPS was a party that throughout the country embodied the anti-Mobutu and pro-change sentiments during the 1980s and 1990s, the party had been reduced to its Kasaian origins. This trend was strengthened by the fact that the opposition parties often do not have an ideological profile, a social project or programmes that distinguish them clearly from other parties. One of the rare exceptions was Vital Kamerhe's UNC, which capitalized on its leader's period of silence after his departure as president of the National Assembly in order to deepen his political vision, which was partially inspired by the left-wing populism of Latin America, particularly that of Brazil. The parties are often relatively young and have not had the time to establish themselves at grassroots level and to put in place clear and solid structures, which obviously does not facilitate internal democracy.

There has never been a tradition in Central Africa in which the opposition's role has been considered as positive, constructive or essential for democracy and the functioning of the state. On the contrary, the opposition is seen as potentially destabilizing, subversive and threatening. This stigmatization does not facilitate the creation of a broad alliance with other groups in society, such as trade unions and social movements, which were very important in the genesis of a countermovement in the West. Furthermore, there are very few examples in the region of regime changes in which an opposition party has managed to beat the ruling party through electoral means.

Most of the opposition parties have had to work with very limited or even non-existent budgets, without access to the state's financial and logistical means to conduct their campaign. Their candidates were not able to make the same number of visits to their grassroots, were not able to distribute as many small gifts (t-shirts, caps, drinks), and could not provide the same quantities of beer and cold drinks at their rallies. This is one of the reasons why opposition parties find it difficult to access rural areas. They are active on the political scene in cities and present in the press, but hardly at all in rural areas, which may give them a distorted idea of their own popularity. Though they can mobilize many people in the places they visit, there is a tendency to extrapolate this mobilization to places they have not visited.

Opposition parties were strictly held to what the electoral law prescribed as the campaign period, while the ruling parties started their campaign months before the official period. In fact, Kabila was in campaign mode from when he used the *Cinquantenaire* as the launch pad for his re-election. The opposition parties, entering the ring with unequal weapons, were not able to capitalize on the sense of Kabila fatigue that existed amongst a large part of the electorate.

In mid-December 2010 Kamerhe announced that he would run for the presidency as the candidate of the UNC and left the next day for the east. A huge and noisy crowd gathered in Goma and his hometown Bukavu. That did not mean he would win the elections, but at least made clear that the 2011 elections would be entirely different from those in 2006. Kabila had won those elections because of widespread support for him in the east. Now that his 2006 campaign leader had decided to run against him things would never be the same again.

Kabila continued to consider himself irreplaceable. He knew he had lost much of his popularity, which he believed he could easily win back through accelerated infrastructural works and a good campaign. Kamerhe was also overwhelmed by the enthusiastic masses he had mobilized, and thought that the anti-Kabila sentiment among the general public was so strong that the electorate would automatically vote for him. But many people remained suspicious as to why this flamboyant man, who had gone to the four corners of the country to explain why they should vote for Kabila, now proclaimed the opposite. An important part of public opinion in the west of Congo simply did not believe that Kamerhe really wanted to rally against his former friend, and did not rule out his so-called opposition being simply a strategy to divide and confuse the opposition.

Also in December 2010, on the other side of the country, the old anti-Mobutu opposition icon, Etienne Tshisekedi, had made his own glorious entry into Kinshasa after years of absence to confirm his participation in the presidential elections. People gathered in massive crowds to welcome him. Tshisekedi was born in 1932 in the Kasai, in the south-central Congo. He joined Mobutu and became a minister in several of his governments. For many years he was a prominent member of the executive bureau of the MPR and was considered one of the architects of Mobutism.

Relations with Mobutu ruptured around 1980. Tshisekedi led a dissident group against Mobutu as one of thirteen MPs who published a critical open letter. In February 1982, they founded the UDPS. A few weeks later, Tshisekedi was arrested, which marked the beginning of many years in and out of prison and house arrest. Despite this persecution, the UDPS managed to spread rapidly throughout the country. Tshisekedi was the most important political leader during the *Conférence Nationale Souveraine*, inviting 2,000 delegates representing the country's various social, political and geographic interests. Its mandate was to agree on a blueprint for the country's future. In August 1992, the CNS appointed Tshisekedi prime minister, but that was quickly overruled by Mobutu's counter-government.

When the war broke out, Tshisekedi failed to recognize the relevance of this new development and never tried to talk with the rebels. They never called him either, and he faded from the political scene. In 2002, he returned as a delegate to the Inter-Congolese Dialogue at Sun City. He refused to sign the final agreement and went to Kigali to negotiate with RCD-Goma, which also had not signed the agreement. This, of course, alienated him from many people in the east of Congo. The UDPS did not participate in the transitional government or the 2006 elections. It was a little unfortunate that the self-declared champion of democracy in Congo had chosen not to participate in the first multiparty elections in the country in four decades. But now he was back. His party could no longer mobilize people in the entire country, but Tshisekedi had kept his popularity intact in Kinshasa and the two Kasai provinces.

Bemba, meanwhile, was not in the picture. Even in the very unlikely case of him being freed before the elections, the MLC leader and former vice-president of Congo would not have been able to register as a candidate. However he remained the political heir of Mobutism, with its roots in the north-western province of Equateur. The most important personalities in that part of the political landscape were the late president's son Nzanga Mobutu and the old survivor Kengo wa Dondo. Nzanga had been Kabila's coalition partner in 2006 but the alliance with Kabila came to an end in March 2011. Kengo is a skilled and cunning politician, born in 1930 to a Congolese mother and a Polish father. He had been Mobutu's prime minister on three separate occasions and maintained himself in the political arena by using his refined political intuition and insight. In 2007, he was able to manoeuvre himself into the seat of speaker of the Senate despite the fact that, formally, he belonged to the opposition.

A crucial but unanswered question was: what exactly was the capacity of the opposition to mobilize the people, not in the polling booths but for rallies and demonstrations in the street? The UDPS especially seemed to believe it was capable of organizing massive marches in the capital and other cities. The question was also: would the opposition, in the event that it was actually capable of mobilizing the masses, be able to manage the potential violence stemming from the frustration of citizens who, at the end of the first legislature, found themselves living under the same conditions as before 2006. The progress made in infrastructure and at the macroeconomic level was not felt at a grassroots level. This anger gave massive rallies and demonstrations an unpredictable edge.

The Congolese public followed the events of the Arab Spring with great interest throughout 2011, but the context in the DRC was different. The middle classes that had initiated the changes in North Africa hardly existed in Congo. Social media and ICT, which played an important role in the Arab Spring, were much less accessible in Congo. The precarious economic conditions in which people lived in Congo made it impossible to demonstrate for weeks. In fact the daily struggle for most people was so hard that it was out of the question for them to demonstrate for more than two or three days. But most of all, it was difficult to imagine that a fast-growing counterforce could happen in Congo without excessive violence by the forces of order.

The campaign was harsh and the speeches aggressive, more so than in 2006.[6] Since March 2011, Human Rights Watch (HRW) has documented dozens of events or forums where candidates called on their supporters to commit violence or deployed ethnic hate speech. Security forces have used unnecessary or excessive force against demonstrators even at ordinary rallies. This all contributed to a climate of fear around the elections.[7] In Kinshasa the phrase circulated: 'Si Kabila perd, c'est la guerre' ('If Kabila loses, it will be war'). This obviously affected the credibility of the elections.

The technical preparation of the process was no help to the credibility of the elections either: all steps were taken with delays. The CENI had been installed too late, and the registration of voters had been very controversial. Neither the new electoral law, nor the voters' list, nor the budget were ready.[8] One month before the elections, it was unlikely that they would be held on the scheduled day, but with logistical support from South Africa, CENI accelerated its preparations.

In the end, the elections of 28 November took place with many irregularities. Electoral rolls and polling stations were a total mess, and numerous people were unable to reach the place they were supposed to vote following the late display and lack of notification regarding voters' rolls. Many others were not able to vote and/or had to vote late due to the late opening of polling stations following the delayed arrival or lack of electoral materials. The large number of political party witnesses made the voting process difficult at many polling stations, since these witnesses had not been properly trained. In some places, voters and local CENI agents were intimidated, and sensitive election materials, particularly ballot papers, were not properly secured. Generally, there was a lack of training of the electoral personnel to maintain full control over the procedures, and huge ignorance on the part of the electorate about the entire process, due to electoral and civic education being largely inadequate.[9]

The Carter Center reported that the tabulation process in Kinshasa and Lubumbashi was problematic. Sensitive materials arrived by various means of transport, both official and private; were handled haphazardly, sometimes with bags and results envelopes opened; were stockpiled outside with insufficient or no protection from the elements (after a rain storm results forms were found hanging on sticks to dry); heads of polling centres were observed opening sealed envelopes with results forms and completing or altering paperwork in breach of procedure. Coupled with the general disorganization of these centres, a significant number of polling station results were lost.[10]

The elections had been badly organized with a lot of irregularities, but not to the same extent everywhere. Especially in Katanga, the Province Orientale and Bandundu results were so unlikely that they torpedoed the credibility of the process. On Katanga for instance, the Carter Center wrote in its press release:

> Based on the detailed results released by CENI, it is also evident that multiple locations, notably several Katanga province constituencies, reported impossibly high rates of 99 to 100% voter turnout with all, or nearly all, votes going to incumbent President Joseph Kabila. These and other observations point to mismanagement of the results process and compromise the integrity of the presidential election.

I spent those days in Bukavu, where the polling had been very quiet and at first sight impeccable. But I talked to a fifteen-year-old girl in the house where I stayed: she had managed to be registered on the electoral list despite being four years too young. She voted, walked out of the polling station and thought: 'That was fun! Let's try it again.' She walked into another station and voted again.

Before, during and after polling day, the situation was very tense in the DRC, particularly in Kinshasa. The announcement of results, originally planned for 6 December, was postponed. The CENI electoral commission published the results as and when they were compiled, before proclaiming, on the afternoon of 9 December, Joseph Kabila's victory with 48.95% of the vote. Etienne Tshisekedi, in second place with 32.33% of the vote, rejected these results and proclaimed himself the president elect. Vital Kamerhe came third, gaining 7.75% of the vote.

For the first few weeks after the proclamation, the situation in Kinshasa remained explosive. The 'president elect' called upon the population to protest, but the streets of Kinshasa were cordoned off by security forces and Tshisekedi's home was under constant surveillance. Human Rights Watch reported at least twenty-four people killed by the security forces and dozens arbitrarily detained in the days following the announcement of Kabila's victory on 9 December,[11] including opposition activists and supporters as well as people gathered on the street or even in their homes.

Even though the results of the elections remained contested, the chances that the country would implode gradually decreased as neither the cancellation of the elections, nor the reissuing of electoral operations, nor the recounting of votes were seen as serious options. The chaotic way in which the ballot papers had been handled after 28 November made a recount technically impossible.

The legislative elections had complicated the situation even more, in terms of the way they were held (with numerous irregularities) and their results: a very heterogeneous Parliament, with a landscape that was split into two camps, majority and opposition parties, each a mosaic of big, smaller, tiny and one-man parties.

The new majority counted at least sixty factions, including some baronies led by government ministers. The PPRD remained the first party, with 130 MPs, only 55% of the seats it obtained in

2006. This meant that the partners in the majority became more important. The AFDC (*Alliance des Forces Démocratiques du Congo*) of Modeste Bahati obtained seventeen MPs, and Pierre Lumbi's MSR thirty-two. Both parties managed to maintain a certain degree of independence within the majority and counted a number of people with a civil society background in their ranks. They had used civil society methods to organize their structure and their campaign, and started to harvest the fruits of it. The *Alliance pour le Renouveau du Congo* (ARC) of Kabila's minister of planning, Olivier Kamitatu, obtained sixteen MPs. The *Parti Lumumbiste Unifié* (PALU) suffered a heavy loss. Antoine Gizenga had played an important role in 2006 by asking his voters after the first round of the presidential elections to vote for Kabila for the second round, and had been rewarded with the post of prime minister, but he was too old to participate actively in the 2011 campaign. Different factions were openly fighting each other and Adolphe Muzito, who succeeded him in October 2008, was known for bad governance and extensive personal enrichment. The *Parti du Peuple pour la Paix et la Démocratie* (PPPD), created in September as a satellite party of PPRD in an attempt to anticipate the anti-PPRD/anti-Kabila feeling within the electorate, obtained twenty-nine seats in Parliament. This mosaic made it much more complicated than in 2006 to install a stable government.[12] It was also worth noting that only seventy-eight MPs elected in 2006 were able to renew their mandate.

In addition, the opposition was more divided than in 2006. Without Bemba, the MLC had obtained a much less impressive result: twenty-two seats instead of sixty-six in 2006. Its leadership in Kinshasa was paralysed by the shadow of Bemba, who remained the party leader and took the major decisions from his prison cell in The Hague. Kamerhe's UNC, a newcomer in the Parliament, obtained eighteen seats, a lot given that the party had been created only one year ahead of the elections and jumped into the arena without substantial financial means. But many people had expected more.

Because of its boycott in 2006, the UDPS was also a newcomer in Parliament, becoming the most significant player in the opposition with forty-two seats (obtained by candidates who did not have financial support for their campaigns). This impressive result was, however, offset by Tshisekedi's political stand. He refused to recognize his defeat and considered the elections and the resulting institutions illegitimate. He forbade his elected MPs to take up their mandate as long as he had not been inaugurated as president of the DRC. Most of them eventually did so regardless, considering this the only possible way to play the historical role the party had always claimed but never played. Tshisekedi's attitude not only hindered the deployment of a coherent and collective opposition, it also weakened the UDPS in the eyes of the electorate.

The DRC had, in 2006, completed its complex peace process with the organization of elections labelled by various observers as sufficiently fair and free. The 2011 elections, by contrast, were not held to consolidate democracy but to consolidate power.[13]

The West was very ambiguous in the signals it sent. Though Western countries insisted on holding the elections, they then went quite far in accepting undemocratic practices. This behaviour is partially explained by the search for a delicate balance between the desire to contribute to the development of democracy on the one hand, and on the other the concern not to damage stability, which remained precarious. Of course such pragmatism is also based on a solid understanding by each of the international players of its own bilateral interests. The ambiguity of the Congo's Western partners is well understood, by both political players in the region and the local population. But this means international partners become the most important source of legitimacy.

After two elections, Congo had state institutions, values and a system borrowed from the West, with an elected president, a legislative body, a government to execute power, a constitution, an army and an administration, expressing itself in the jargon of democracy and development which is a condition for a regime to be accepted at international negotiation tables.

But underneath the surface, patrimonial and predatory-style pork-barrel governance continues to be the norm. Clientelism had shaped the democratization process in its own image much more than democracy had managed to influence the logics and rigour of clientelism; and public funds were still rerouted to those in power who desperately needed them to maintain their clients.[14]

Michael Deibert is very severe in his judgement, but I entirely agree with it:

> Joseph Kabila's government remains, in many ways, a younger, more sophisticated, more polished version of his father's, relying on an extremely narrow circle of trusted individuals and a network of international alliances to keep itself at the top of those scrambling for control of Congo. It is a power structure that has built a patronage base rather than a political base on which it can draw. It has not created institutional structures that will resolve Congo's underlying issues.[15]

Kabila continued to govern a conflict-torn country where not only the landscape of armed groups was atomized, but the political caste was also splintered into many micro-parties, breakaway factions or very small groups. It remained very difficult to build stable coalitions in this political environment.

The international partners had not been able to bring positive change. This was confirmed in the report of the European Court of Auditors in September 2013 examining EU support between the start of the transition in 2003 and Kabila's re-election in 2011. The court concluded that the effectiveness of EU assistance for governance in the DRC had been very limited, although the support had been set within a generally sound cooperation strategy, addressed the main needs and had achieved some results. But fewer than half the programmes examined had delivered, without much prospect for sustainability.[16] The West happily believed that it had contributed to the rehabilitation of the Congolese state, but neither two elections (2006 and 2011) nor years of army reforms had allowed it to rise from the ashes.

In the eyes of the Congolese population, the West has lost all credibility. Despite lip service paid to democracy, the people did not feel a real commitment and the main challenges were not addressed: bad governance and poverty remained endemic; land and identity issues were still a time bomb; and the Congolese state remained fragile, without the capacity or political will to reform the instruments needed to guarantee the rule of law.

The regime survived the elections of 2011 but two big questions remained. Firstly, what were Kabila's plans beyond 2016? Nobody knew if he intended to enter his new mandate with the aim of handing over power to an elected successor in 2016, as required by the constitution, or if he envisaged maintaining his rule beyond constitutional limits. Also, it was unclear whether the entire regime would support him should he choose the latter option. Kamerhe's dissidence had shown that the regime lacked coherence. Secondly, what would be the consequences of a polarized military landscape in Kivu? Elections are often considered a very uncertain period because of rising inter- and intra-community tensions. The immediate consequence is that armed groups, anticipating trouble, remobilize, recruit and acquire arms. This reinforced military landscape had not yet been set in motion in 2011, but the question in early 2012 was how this polarized situation would evolve.

Chapter 6

THE M23 MISADVENTURE

The Terminator on the run

After the contested election of November 2011, Congo remained a sort of twilight zone in the early months of 2012, politically as well as due to the military situation in the east. The political landscape was totally divided, with discord inside the majority, a complete lack of cohesion within the opposition and no communication at all between the two.

Several events then created an entirely new situation. On 12 February 2012 Katumba Mwanke died in a plane crash. In the same period, Bosco Ntaganda, the CNDP leader and since the *Umoja Wetu* campaign the pillar of Kabila's regime in Kivu, left his post and hid in Rutshuru. On 18 April 2012 outgoing finance minister Augustin Matata Ponyo was appointed prime minister. And by the end of the month it was clear that Congo had to deal with a new Tutsi-led rebellion, the M23.

Katumba had managed to become the leading personality inside Kabila's inner circle after the death of Samba Kaputo (2007), Vital Kamerhe's fall from grace (2009) and John Numbi's suspension because of his alleged involvement in the murder of Floribert Chebeya (2010). He rarely met with Western diplomats but played an important role in the establishment and management of Kabila's private economic empire. He was very familiar with the Rwandan regime as one of the architects of *Umoja Wetu*, and also connected to governmental and business networks in South Africa, where he had lived for some years after Mobutu's departure. He was also close to Dan Gertler, the Israeli trader with interests in gold and copper mining and close links to the Kabila family. In Congo he was known as the kingmaker behind the scenes and the man with the key to the state's treasury. As a member of a small community in South Katanga, he played a crucial role in managing the mineral resources and tensions between the richer southern part of the province and the north, which felt abandoned. Most importantly of all, he monopolized access to the president.

Augustin Katumba Mwanke took so much space in the functioning of the Congolese state that the gaping hole left after his death was comparable to the impact of a meteorite crater: it reshaped the entire landscape. Immediately after his passing, speculation started to circulate as to who would replace him. Several politicians tried to occupy the space left by Katumba but nobody succeeded, and in the months after his death it became increasingly clear he had not been replaced. Instead, the president himself seized the momentum to grow in his role and to give greater weight to his family: his wife Olive Lemba, his twin sister Jaynet Kabila and his younger brother Zoe Kabila. The latter two had been elected as MPs three months earlier.

Katumba Mwanke died when the regime was in deep crisis. With him, the last vestige of collectivity disappeared from the process of decision-making at the top of the regime. He enjoyed the confidence of the president and had the ability to coach him. After Katumbe Mwanke's death, Kabila relied on individuals for specific dossiers and thus created a situation where he was the only person with an overview. Several collaborators have told me that when Katumba disappeared Kabila became a ship without a radar.[1] And Congo too.

Meanwhile, in Kinshasa, Kabila was under a lot of pressure from his international partners, who were not amused by the election's lack of credibility. Irregularities and violence had undermined its legitimacy, but re-counting the votes was not realistic and organizing new elections even less so. Kabila thought it would be a convincing move to appoint a prime minister from the opposition, but that was not easy. Many inside the majority had the ambition of becoming prime minister themselves, and there was no obvious opposition leader to do the job. Kengo wa Dondo and Vital Kamerhe both had difficulties being recognized as genuine opposition figures by at least a section of public opinion, and Etienne Tshisekedi[2] was convinced that, someday soon, the army would come to his house and take him to the presidential palace as the true winner of the elections, a scenario even those in his own party did not believe. So the outgoing government remained in charge.

But there was a less difficult option for Kabila to show his goodwill to the international community, signalling that the elections were a mistake and that he remained dedicated to democracy and human rights: delivering Bosco Ntaganda to the International Criminal Court in The Hague. Bosco Ntaganda had sealed the marriage of convenience between Kagame and Kabila at the start of *Umoja Wetu*, but Western partners had condemned his nomination as chief of operations of the FARDC in eastern Congo after the integration of the CNDP into the army, because there was an international arrest warrant against him. Furthermore, in 2009 Ntaganda had been the only option to replace Laurent Nkunda as leader of the CNDP. But Nkunda's disappearance had widened the rifts inside the Congolese Tutsi community and Ntaganda had never been accepted by the entire ex-rebel movement.[3]

Since 2009, Ntaganda had become gradually involved in the trafficking of natural resources, working together with General Gabriel Amisi, also known as Tango Four. Amisi had an RCD background and knew most of the CNDP because they had served under him during the war. By broadening his business network and activities, Bosco unavoidably clashed with the interests of leading officers in the Congolese and the Rwandan armies.[4] In short, everybody had good reasons to get rid of Bosco. He was an obvious scapegoat and easy to sacrifice. But rumours of his imminent arrest were leaked and Bosco left Goma, withdrawing into the hills of Rutshuru with a small group of heavily armed confidants.

On 18 April, Kabila appointed Augustin Matata Ponyo as his prime minister. This was perceived by many international observers as a brilliant move. Matata had made a career as a financial expert and economist. He worked for the *Banque Centrale du Congo* (BCC), had been on many training courses and had represented his country internationally at the IMF. A new institution was created in 2003, the *Bureau Central de Coordination* (Bececo). Matata was appointed director-general, and managed the funding from international donors for national reconstruction. He served under Muzito as minister of finance from February 2010 onwards and took credit for the macro-economic successes, including the follow-up of the debt relief granted to the DRC under the Heavily Indebted Poor Countries programme after the achievement of its completion points in June 2010, including the stabilization of the Congolese franc, the introduction of VAT and some legal reforms of public finances and customs. This record gave Matata an aura of being the right man in the right place for diplomats and the international financial institutions.

On the Congolese political scene, he was considered a technocrat, somebody who could give the public the feeling that the country was in good hands while the unresolved political questions were kept on hold. This impression was reinforced when on 28 April he installed his government, with a mix of relatively unknown newcomers and some old celebrities from the past, but without the party presidents within the presidential majority and other heavyweights. Two deputy prime ministers, twenty-five ministers and eleven vice-ministers were appointed, but Pierre Lumbi of MSR was not given ministerial responsibilities despite good results in the elections. The ARC leader Olivier Kamitatu was not included in the government either. The most notable of the absent politicians was Evariste Boshab, the outgoing speaker of Parliament who had openly claimed the post of prime minister. Many had expected that Kabila would appoint at least some opposition members, but he did not. Four Rwandophone ministers were appointed, two Hutu and two Tutsi.

The new prime minister Matata Ponyo and the new speaker of Parliament Aubin Minaku represented a new generation. Both were born in 1964. By appointing them, Kabila rewarded the two provinces where voting had been beyond expectations: Bandundu (Minaku) and Maniema (Matata).

The situation was not only confused in Kinshasa, but also in the eastern provinces. The CNDP's inclusion in the army after *Umoja Wetu* alienated a lot of non-Rwandophone soldiers who had difficulty understanding how they were supposed to obey the rebels they had been fighting until recently. Several officers deserted with part of the troops they commanded. New armed groups were created. Existing armed groups reinforced themselves through new recruitments.

Not only did new groups emerge, a new kind of mobilization occurred in the rural areas of Kivu. An interesting example was *Raia Mutomboki* ('Outraged Citizens'), which had been created in 2005 in the remote areas of Shabunda, and remained for years under the international radar because its impact was limited to the very local level, with no established links to provincial or national politics. But after *Umoja Wetu*, *Raia Mutomboki* started to grow and became one of the biggest and best organized armed groups, an attempt by frustrated citizens to protect themselves in an environment where the Congolese state could not manage local conflicts or neutralize the FDLR, and where the national army was not only more part of the problem than the solution, but was led by Tutsi officers. The backbone of the movement was a mixture of young unemployed rural youngsters, former militia members and deserters, with support from the customary authorities and other community leaders.[5]

Raia Mutomboki spread, not as a military organization with a clear structure or chain of command, but more as a brand, where local groups took the name and the spirit, 'more a franchise than a unitary force', making use of the same fetishes which were used by earlier generations of Mai Mai groups to make themselves seem invulnerable.[6]

One year before the 2011 elections, the CNDP had entered the presidential majority and became the pillar on which Kabila relied for his re-election. They supported his campaign with intimidation and violence, and in many areas they prevented opposition candidates and parties organizing rallies. Particularly in the territory of Masisi, the elections were manipulated.

The 2011 elections would define the contours of power for years. Ethnic relations polarized, especially on the land issue. Traditional land conflicts were aggravated because of the greed of the *nouveaux riches* who had emerged during the wars and conflict since the 1990s, and because of the repatriation of Rwandophone Congolese citizens who were resettled in Kivu. In some cases, people were transplanted to places in Congo which had never had a Rwandophone community. The programme was considered by many as a plan for the repopulation of Kivu by Rwandan citizens, to cope with Rwanda's demographic pressure.

The pre-electoral tensions accelerated recruitment by the armed groups. Throughout 2011, the political/military landscape in the Kivus was tense but relatively calm. Communities and armed groups mobilized and positioned themselves in the elections, awaiting the results and the political, administrative and military configurations that would take shape as a result. But the military landscape changed rapidly in the first months of 2012, triggered by Bosco Ntaganda's flight. An army unit was sent out to arrest him. Somebody close to Kabila told me that Bosco was never arrested because there was no common vision about what should be done afterwards, even though all parties involved agreed on the need to neutralize him. Nobody was enthusiastic about the idea of delivering him to the ICC in The Hague.[7]

Meanwhile, Bosco Ntaganda was leading a battle that he could not win. He was isolated but still had a considerable capacity to cause trouble. In early April 2012, 300 soldiers defected and joined him, the majority of them with a CNDP background. The rebels chose the name *Mouvement du 23 mars*, which refers to the peace agreement of 23 March 2009.[8] The rebels took up arms because of what they considered to be the government's lack of political will in implementing the agreement, including the requirement of officers to maintain their military grade within the CNDP when they joined the army. Poor living conditions in the army were an additional grievance.

But probably the most important reason for the creation of M23 was the fact that Kabila had to prove to the nation and the entire world that he was capable of dismantling the army within the army, the state within the state. Despite all the statements about successful integration, the CNDP continued to exist as a separate structure with its own administration and chain of command. The key element here was the relocation of the CNDP, sending its soldiers out of the Kivus and into other regions, spreading them among units where they were mixed in with soldiers from other parts of the country. This is essential for true integration, and as long as this was not done the CNDP remained an army inside an army. Since 2009, this relocation had met a great deal of resistance among the CNDP's ranks, and for years was one of the ultimate taboos for the CNDP leadership. Shortly after that, Sultani Makenga, a forty-year-old Tutsi colonel with the reputation of being a good fighter and strategist, joined M23. Makenga was loyal to Laurent Nkunda and had served in the Rwandan army, but was also known to be against too much Rwandan influence in North Kivu. Others followed his move. Within a few days, the rebel movement became much stronger.

In any case, another Tutsi-led uprising was born. As with previous movements, M23 had roots in the Congolese Tutsi community and its historical grievances. The leadership of all these movements was in the hands of Congolese Tutsi officers with support from Kigali, which had a highly politicized agenda. Not only was the relationship between the Congolese Tutsi and the Rwandan capital turbulent, the community in Congo as well as the political elite of Rwanda were deeply divided. Many young Congolese Tutsi had joined the RPF in their struggle against the Habyarimana regime (1990–1994) and stayed when the RPF started the two wars on Congolese soil (1996–1997 and 1998–2002), no longer as RPF soldiers but as officers of the Rwandan-backed rebels. But soon some of them began to distrust the Rwandan regime because they thought the Congolese Tutsi were being manipulated by a purely Rwandan agenda, while their specific perspective as a Congolese community was not being taken into account. The legendary General Patrick (Pacifique) Masunzu, for instance, a Munyamulenge from the highlands around Minembwe in South Kivu, had joined the RPF in 1991, fought in the second war as a RCD-Goma officer (1998–1999) but separated from the RCD in 1999 because he refused to fight a war on behalf of Rwanda. He started his own armed group against the RCD and the Rwandan army, forming coalitions with Congolese Mai Mai groups. After the war, he became Kabila's trump card to reassure the Tutsi from South Kivu, the Banyamulenge, that they had a place in the Democratic Republic of Congo and was rewarded with the lucrative and powerful position of commander of 10 Military Region based in Bukavu. He kept that position until September 2014. Several insiders of FARDC's elite suggested that his removal was related to his alleged involvement in the massacre of Mutarule.

Earlier Tutsi-led rebellions had been able to mobilize nearly the entire Rwandophone community of Congo – i.e. the Tutsi communities of North and South Kivu, each with its own history, tradition and relationship to Kigali – as well as the Hutu community, which is particularly strong in Rutshuru and Masisi in North Kivu, and even important leaders within some of the other ethnic communities. This was the result of a Rwandan policy to create a communal alliance. The nearly uncontested leadership of Eugène Serufuli, former governor of North Kivu and economic heavyweight in the province, was a cornerstone in Hutu support for the RCD-Goma and later for the CNDP.

But the mobilization capacity of M23 turned out to be considerably lower. Serufuli stayed loyal to Kinshasa, very few Hutus joined

M23 and an important segment of the Tutsi also refused to come on board. The Banyamulenge leaders distanced themselves from M23 from the start, and went into the communities to explain that this war was not their war. The political wing of the movement, much less influential than the armed group, was more ethnically diverse, with representatives with different ethnic backgrounds, although most of them had little legitimacy in their communities.

The failing mobilization obviously had a negative impact on the military range of the movement. The M23 started with 300 combatants and this figure grew to 1,000–2,500.[9] But that was not enough to conquer and hold territory. They limited themselves to the destabilization of parts of Rutshuru. Much of their weaponry came from arms caches which CNDP officers had hidden in 2009, before integrating into the FARDC.[10] Although the group had relatively few combatants, they were well-organized and well-armed, and resisted relatively easily the threat from unmotivated FARDC soldiers deployed in chaotic conditions with sometimes unclear chains of command.

Of course, the key question immediately after the creation of M23 was: what was the exact involvement of Rwanda and to a lesser extent Uganda in this fresh outburst of violence? The first evidence was provided by the UN Group of Experts on the DRC, based on interviews with M23 deserters, ex-CNDP soldiers who had chosen to remain in the FARDC and local eye-witnesses. Afterwards, the conclusions of the GoE were confirmed by the investigations undertaken by MONUSCO and Human Rights Watch.[11]

Initially, Kigali had been facilitating contact between different CNDP leaders, Bosco Ntaganda and Nkunda loyalist Sultani Makenga in the first instance, to enable them to join forces, and helped them organize recruitment to the new armed group. High-ranking Rwandan officials addressed Tutsi community leaders in meetings M23 organized in Rwanda to create a broad base of support. In later stages, Rwandan army officials intervened through military support for M23, with permanent troop reinforcements and even joint operations in Rutshuru. Rwandan officers provided M23 with weapons, communication equipment and medical support, including evacuating injured combatants to Rwanda for treatment. Recruitment for M23 has continued in Rwandan villages, former CNDP officers have joined the rebellion on Rwandan territory and RPF members have collected funds for the movement.[12]

When it became clear that Rwanda was very actively supporting M23, it was heavily criticized by some of its most loyal bilateral partners. In Washington, London, The Hague, Berlin and Stockholm immediate measures were taken to cut or suspend parts of their bilateral support. These measures clearly hit Rwanda where it hurts and also had an important discouraging effect in Congo itself (individuals and groups thought twice before joining M23) and in Uganda, which retained a lower profile and acted with greater discretion than Rwanda in its support for the rebel movement.

Senior officials of the Ugandan government had also provided support to M23 in the form of direct troop reinforcements in Congolese territory, weapons deliveries, technical assistance, joint planning, political advice and facilitation of external relations. Units of the Ugandan People's Defence Forces and the Rwandan Defence Forces jointly supported M23 in a series of attacks in July 2012 to take over the major towns of Rutshuru territory and the Congolese armed forces base of Rumangabo. But the most important Ugandan contribution to the growth of M23 was the facilities the rebels were granted to establish their political branch in Kampala and to implement their rather professional communication strategy which boosted the movement's external relations.[13]

For both Rwanda and Uganda, there was clear evidence that M23 was supported by officials and officers who held strategic positions in the army and the state, but it was extremely difficult to determine to what extent that support was the result of government policy or the result of decisions by key people within the regime. However it obviously affected the legitimacy of Yoweri Museveni in his role as chairman of the International Conference on the Great

Lakes Region (ICGLR), an intergovernmental organization established in 2004 uniting Kenya, Congo and Congo's nine immediate neighbours. Since the division of Sudan, South Sudan had become the twelfth member. The ICRGL's mandate was based on the recognition that political instability and conflicts in and between its member states had a considerable regional dimension and thus required a concerted effort in order to promote sustainable peace and development. The ICGLR was and still is a very young structure, and for the time being its greatest merit is that it exists.

The genesis of M23 was, to some extent, apparently irrational. It is not clear what Rwanda or the Congolese Tutsi elite could gain through this new crisis. Since 2009 the CNDP had become much larger, controlling many more troops, a considerably greater geographical area and more strategic sites – especially in its capacity to exploit natural resources. Whatever the outcome of the M23 crisis, it was unlikely that the Congolese Tutsi elite would maintain the same level of control. Also Rwanda's motivation in launching itself into this new adventure was difficult to understand. Since *Umoja Wetu* in January 2009, Kagame had appeared to be Kabila's most reliable partner. With the elections in view, Kabila knew that his army would never be able to maintain the necessary stability in the east of Congo. Kagame seemed to be the only person who could keep the violence in Kivu at a manageable level. Kagame also needed to maintain his good relationship with Kabila in order to prevent military action against his regime taking shape on Congolese soil, especially after the defection of Kayumba Nyamwasa in March 2010. Through its alliance with the CNDP, Rwanda could maintain its control over the exploitation and traffic of minerals, and continue to use Congo as a safety-valve against the demographic pressure structurally prevalent within its own borders. The improved relationship between Kagame and Kabila turned out to be advantageous for both men, but the fact that the Rwandan state was much stronger compared to the fragile Congolese state made this alliance a very unequal partnership.

The military landscape that had formed in 2011 now exploded into action. M23 tried to forge alliances with existing armed groups, directly under the command of Ntaganda and Makenga, to facilitate the expansion of M23 and impede the FARDC operations against M23. Also in Ituri, M23 reached out to different local armed groups in order to organize them against the government. Here, though, they failed. Other armed groups also operationalized their combatants to defend themselves against M23. FDLR, for instance, attacked by the FARDC as well as M23, committed abuses against civilians.[14]

Bosco's rebellion and the foundation of M23 seemed to be stillborn. It was not an instrument for a new war or a means to obtain power, but rather an attempt to force new negotiations and obtain a better position within the army and the government. M23 had a very negative local impact: HRW and other international human rights organizations reported crimes against humanity and war crimes in its radius of action, which caused a new wave of internally displaced persons.[15] But the capacity to cause serious trouble was also high due to the internal rot within the army and the total distrust between local communities.

The M23 operations obviously put President Kabila under intense pressure. His unfortunate position had a lot of similarities with the situation in 2008. His government was not able to convince people in the east of Congo of its capacity or even ambition to tackle the root causes of the conflicts in the region. His army was not able to deal with a relatively small armed group. M23 had caught him in a Catch-22 situation: an important part of public opinion was certain to disagree with any negotiations and nobody would believe that they could lead to a sustainable peace. But refusing to negotiate would further marginalize him on the regional and international political scene, and increase military pressure. On top of this, Rwandan support for M23 had made it clear that Kabila had lost his most reliable ally.

The uprising took the attention away from what the new government was doing. Prime Minister Matata's reforms became totally overshadowed by events in the east. Meanwhile, in the army, Kabila was losing his last vestige of credibility. Rumours spread quickly that some parts of the army command and several key officers had issued a kind of ultimatum against Kabila in Kinshasa. The deadline passed without anything happening but these rumours kept on coming back and degenerated later in the year into wild speculations about a forthcoming coup d'état, despite everybody knowing that the army has nothing to contribute to stabilizing the country due to its lack of structure, cohesion and discipline. A coup attempt was doomed to fail and could only create more confusion, as well as a deep constitutional crisis.

The fall of Goma

For months, M23 committed local violence with huge impacts on local communities and national politics, but there was nothing that suggested M23 would bring the country close to another implosion anytime soon. However, on Thursday 15 November that changed, as M23 launched a major attack, firstly on Kibumba and then Goma. It was such a large offensive that it went way beyond M23's own military capacity. Very soon confirmation was received, through independent sources, of the massive support and even the direct involvement of the Rwandan army in the operation. The first analysis was that M23 did not intend to take Goma. Nkunda had reached the edge of the town in 2008 with the CNDP, but under pressure from Kagame and international diplomacy had not taken it. This seemed the most likely scenario once again. M23 had already experienced several difficult months and putting extreme pressure on Goma looked like the best way to force negotiations from a position of relative strength. Taking the city would have highly significant consequences and the risk of violence and massacres in and around the town would be high, changing the entire outlook of the conflict.

On Sunday 18 November it became obvious that Goma would not resist the attack. Thousands of people fled the town and the surrounding refugee camps. The army and political authorities also left. On Sunday afternoon, as in 2008, the rebels stopped some kilometres short of the town and MONUSCO conducted negotiations with the M23 leadership, who requested immediate and direct negotiations with the Congolese government in Kinshasa. The governor of North Kivu returned to town, order was maintained by MONUSCO and the Congolese police. It looked like the worst had been avoided.

But M23 resumed fighting on Monday morning, and Goma fell on Tuesday 20 November. The next day they took Sake, 25 km to the west. Many people expected this to be the first step in an advance south to take Bukavu, as Nkunda had done in 2004 with disastrous consequences for the population, but that did not happen. M23 turned north and further west, consolidating positions in Masisi. The FARDC 'reorganized' itself in Minova, a market town on the border between North and South Kivu. But 'reorganize' was a euphemism for what really happened: According to Human Rights Watch 'En route and in Minova and surrounding communities, the soldiers engaged in a 10-day frenzy of destruction: looting homes, razing shops and shelters in camps for displaced people, and raping at least 76 women and girls'.[16]

On 23 November Kabila had replaced the commander in chief of his land forces, General Gabriel Amisi, the infamous Tango Four. Amisi's reputation was based on his very bad human rights record as RCD general during the war, but also on the fact he was one of those army leaders who used military operations as an illegal source of personal income through corruption and trade of weaponry, uniforms and minerals. He remained in charge because of his close ties with the Kabila family. In November 2012, he was held responsible for the fall of Goma, and suspected of leaking highly confidential information on the operations to M23 officers who had served under him in the RCD. He was replaced by General Olengha, who had lived for decades in Germany and had come back to Congo to join Laurent-Désiré Kabila's liberation war.

With M23 taking Goma and Sake and the FARDC fleeing to Minova, many people had taken and abandoned positions. This increased the competition between the smaller armed groups, which were keen to fill the deserted areas to reinforce their own positions. This not only increased tensions between these armed groups, but also between the ethnic communities, the line between them being very thin. While M23 held Goma, the FDLR took the chance to attack two localities in Rwanda, on the border with Congo. These were their first attacks on Rwandan soil for many years. The FDLR, weakened and drastically reduced in numbers, could only do this by making use of corridors created in Rutshuru, relying on demobilized FDLR combatants who had been recruited by M23 under pressure for information on M23 troop movements. These attacks boosted their morale and provided them with new weapons.

The rebels started to leave Goma on Friday 30 November, the tenth day of occupation, taking away everything which was not too heavy or too hot to carry. Before they left, they plundered state institutions, banks, and arms and ammunition depots. They withdrew to the hills, but kept Goma within easy reach. The Congolese police and the FARDC took control of town. By Saturday 1 December, all M23 forces had left except about a hundred rebels at the airport.

Following this, the military situation around the town stagnated. Apart from some repositioning in the hills around North Kivu's capital, the situation remained calm throughout December. All eyes and ears were focused on two things: the direct talks between the government and M23 in Kampala, and the national dialogue Kabila had announced to restore national unity.

M23 had left town because direct negotiations in Kampala were announced under the auspices of the ICGLR. The negotiations started later in December – although 'started' might not be the proper term. Both camps had a delegation on the spot and from time to time they did seem to talk to each other. They exchanged taunts, produced smokescreens and put procedural questions of all sorts on the table. It was not even completely clear what the negotiations should be about. M23's first objective had been to review the agreements of 23 March 2009, but later it sought to frame the negotiations very broadly – they would not only be about the recent violence in North Kivu and an evaluation of the agreements of 23 March, but also address themes such as the elections, the reform of the state and the army, and the main social issues. In the end, talks did take place between the two parties, but more often through the Ugandan facilitator than directly.[17]

The Kampala negotiations progressed painfully slowly. For both parties, just being there seemed more important than actually achieving anything. But both still wanted to show their goodwill and readiness to talk. The government also needed to buy some time, as the fall of Goma had clearly demonstrated the weakness of the national army in the field. The military power balance in North Kivu could only be changed by the arrival of a neutral force, an idea which started to spread rapidly in the corridors of the different international diplomatic fora.

In February 2013, a document was eventually produced whereby both parties evaluated the agreements of 23 March 2009 between the government and CNDP, and recognized that they had not been executed in their entirety. It is a long and technical document acknowledging that twenty-three of the thirty-five points from 2009 had been (or were being) implemented according to the text, while the other twelve have not been executed. This text meant that everyone escaped with their dignity intact: the government had done a lot, while M23 had a point when it said there was much still to do.

Just after M23 left Goma, President Kabila announced a process to increase national unity. Different people and groups started to work on a variety of concepts with divergent motivations. Parts of the opposition saw it as an opportunity to redistribute the cards. Some people within the government saw it more as a consultation on the big challenges lying ahead – a sort of round table, preferably as technical as possible. Congolese civil society, having lost much of its own coherence and impact over the last ten years, was very divided over it too.

The PPRD barons and party apparatchiks around secretary-general Boshab saw this as an excellent occasion to get rid of Prime Minister Augustin Matata Ponyo, who had started to reform the administration, injecting bits of good governance and installing mechanisms of control which went directly against the interests of those who had controlled the state before him.

The 'moderate opposition' wanted to have a political agreement which would give them a place in the government, and the 'radicals' around Tshisekedi used the occasion to state again that everything that followed the elections of November 2011 was illegitimate and counter to the constitution.

The fall of Goma brought the region close to a new escalation and a possible war. A heavy diplomatic offensive was launched with a leading role for UN Secretary-General Ban Ki-moon himself, which materialized in the Peace, Security and Cooperation Framework (PSCF) Agreement for the Great Lakes region. That agreement, signed on 24 February 2013, involved not only Congo and its immediate neighbours, but also the wider region, including SADC and the African Union. Two key elements of the agreement were the appointment of a Special Envoy of the UN for the Great Lakes region (former President of Ireland Mary Robinson) and a reinforcement of the UN force in Congo: a Force Intervention Brigade (FIB). After long discussions between African institutions (ICGLR, SADC, AU) on the one hand and the United Nations and the United States on the other, a final decision was taken to give it the status of a specialized 'intervention brigade' within MONUSCO's existing 19,815 strong force. It would mainly consist of Tanzanians, South Africans and Malawians, 3,000 men altogether. This brigade would 'neutralize and disarm [M23], as well as other Congolese rebels and foreign armed groups in strife-riven eastern Democratic Republic of Congo'.[18] Most of all, it would fundamentally change the balance of military power in the field.

The PSCF Agreement included provisions designed to prevent countries in the region from interfering in each other's affairs, as well as other provisions aimed at encouraging the reinforcement of weak Congolese institutions and fostering greater donor coordination and engagement. The Congolese government committed itself to reforms in the democratic and security sectors, improvements in the fields of governance and human rights, and economic recovery.

On some issues, the PSCF Agreement was relevant. It was the first significant political re-engagement by donors since the transition in 2003–2006, as well as a new peacekeeping strategy. The UN started to relaunch dialogue between the DRC and its neighbours, in particular Rwanda, as well as to press for much-needed reform. It outlined national, regional and international commitments, and it foresaw extensive benchmarking exercises and implementation mechanisms to be worked out. On the other hand, there was nothing new in the agreed reforms. Security sector reform, the consolidation of state authority, decentralization, economic development and social service delivery, reform of government institutions, reconciliation and democratization had been on the table for more than a decade.[19]

The diplomatic process which led to the signature of the Framework Agreement and later to the deployment of the FIB was rather slow because of two bouts of arm-wrestling. The first was between the different African regional institutions and the traditional key players in international diplomacy in which Africa tried to obtain as much ownership as possible of this process, and later, when the practical and operational issues were discussed, between the different African regional institutions themselves.

The Framework Agreement was proposed in December and submitted for signature in Addis Ababa at the African Union Summit in January. At the last minute, South Africa refused to sign due to what it considered to be a lack of transparency in the process. The agreement also proposed expanding the group of African countries actively involved in it (with, among others, Mozambique – presently the chair of SADC). In more operational terms, South

Africa and SADC strongly objected to the way the neutral force would be integrated into the MONUSCO (the UN peacekeeping force already deployed in the DRC) structure.

Once South Africa had blocked the process, Congo also formulated its grievances. Kabila's government strongly objected to any proposal resembling the CIAT. The Congolese also wondered why they should be forced to reform their democratic institutions when countries such as Rwanda and Uganda are not perceived as being particularly exemplary in this regard.

The talks advanced, but painfully slowly. The United States vetoed the possibility of a neutral force outside of MONUSCO, but SADC refused to deploy troops without being in command of the neutral force. A similar struggle took place between the African institutions, with poles of power as diverse as ICGLR, SADC, the East African Community and the African Union further complicated by bilateral affinities or hostilities between individual countries. Eventually, the Framework Agreement was elaborated and proposed by a very small group of people, steered directly by the office of United Nations Secretary-General.[20]

The Congolese government had been humiliated by the fall of Goma, proof of its inability to control its eastern provinces, so Kinshasa expected a lot from the intervention brigade and tried to accelerate its arrival by strengthening rumours about Ugandan and Rwandan troops on Congolese soil. Rwanda had been very actively present when M23 took Goma but had withdrawn its troops immediately afterwards. Since then, Uganda and Rwanda had been monitored very closely, with very little space left for direct intervention. The leaked mid-term report of the UN Group of Experts confirmed that Rwanda was now only providing limited support to M23 and Uganda none at all.

As long as the FIB was not deployed, M23 remained the strongest military player in the field, but that would no longer be the case when the neutral force arrived. So Rwanda and M23 tried to delay or even prevent the arrival of the intervention brigade through a very aggressive discourse against the UN and targeted messages meant to influence public opinion in Tanzania and South Africa, which predicted corpses being sent back to the countries that contributed to the neutral force. Rwanda accused the UN of cooperation with FDLR.

M23's decline did not wait for the deployment of the FIB: soon after the signature of the Framework Agreement, the internal power struggle intensified and turned violent, with the wing commanded by Sultani Makenga finally defeating the rebels loyal to Bosco Ntaganda. On top of the traditional cleavages between the two camps (based on clans within the Tutsi community and regional dissension between Masisi and Rutshuru) was the strategic question of how to position the movement against the background of the Framework Agreement and other negotiations. It was clear that Makenga was much more eager than Bosco to finalize the negotiations with the government and agree to some sort of integration. Bosco knew he had passed a point of no return and that he would never get an honourable, interesting or lucrative position within the army. Immediately after the violence within M23 erupted, it became clear that Rwanda actively pressurized M23 officers to join Makenga's camp as a way to finish a war which had cost Rwanda, as well as Congo, a great deal. It looked as if both countries were searching for a soft ending, which would crystallize around Makenga. By integrating him into the army, they hoped to establish some sort of balance, similar to that which existed after the CNDP integrated with FARDC at the time of *Umoja Wetu* (January 2009) and before M23 took off (April 2012).

These events considerably weakened the movement. The Group of Experts estimated that more than 200 M23 fighters of both factions were killed in the clashes, even more were injured and many others surrendered to MONUSCO and the Congolese army. M23's operational capacity dropped to fewer than 1,500 combatants.

By mid-March it became clear that Bosco's camp was about to collapse in its face-off with Makenga's troops. The pressure increased and the group of people Bosco could rely on, politically or militarily, in Rwanda, Congo or elsewhere was becoming smaller with every passing day. Finally, he had to choose between fighting to the death or surrendering. On 18 March 2013, Bosco Ntaganda walked into the American embassy in Kigali and requested he be delivered to the ICC in The Hague. Bosco had crossed the border hours earlier with a few dozen fighters, where a unit of the Rwandan army was waiting to disarm them.

M23 did not get much time to lick its wounds. Three important developments happened almost at the same time: a process of change within the FARDC, a new leadership in MONUSCO and the deployment of the FIB.

The Congolese army has gone through a kind of metamorphosis since the fall of Goma. For many years, the FARDC was considered to be a heterogeneous, undisciplined, badly trained amalgam of different militias. Whenever there was a problem of armed bandits on the loose, efforts were made to resolve it by 'integrating' them into the 'regular' army, and giving command to the one that had done the most to violate human rights. The many international efforts to assist the Congolese authorities in setting up a defence apparatus capable of guaranteeing the security of the Congolese people had only disappointing impacts.[21] The result was a phantom army which was systematically listed among the most serious violators of human rights. In short, it was an army that was dangerous for everybody except the enemy.

The process of change became visible from July 2013 onwards. In November 2012, General François Olengha replaced General Gabriel Amisi (aka 'Tango Four') as chief of staff of the army's land forces. In February 2013, 115 commanding officers from Ituri, South and North Kivu were called back to Kinshasa on the pretext of a military seminar and kept there. All of them were considered to be much more involved in business activities around the army than in military operations. They were also suspected of lacking loyalty to the national cause, with their involvement in different local commercial, ethnic and other networks making it impossible for them to provide effective leadership. The replacement of General Mayala Vainqueur by General Lucien Bauma as commander of the military region that covers North Kivu was also very important.

Their disappearance from the field improved a lot of practical issues: the logistics became better organized, uniforms, arms and ammunition were available where and when they were needed and salaries were paid. The first successes gave a boost to the army and created a wave of solidarity with the army among the population, something which was previously unheard of. In contrast to Amisi's period of command, the best trained and equipped battalions were deployed on the front line and made a significant difference – providing evidence that international efforts to reinforce the army were not all bad.

A Congolese army that could carry out successful operations was an important development, but successful reform of the security sector was something else. The army went through a process of change and the challenge was to consolidate it in North Kivu and extend it to the rest of the country. That never happened, but it did make the difference in the war against M23.

Another process of change was witnessed within MONUSCO. Since its deployment, the UN peacekeeping mission had never given the impression it could fulfil its mission and protect the Congolese people. The Blue Helmets were considered non-proactive with a rather vague role, never there when the events that mattered happened, lacking in-depth knowledge of Congo, its cultures and its history, and thus incapable of understanding the complex conflict dynamics they were supposed to manage. Moreover, they were regarded as enthusiastic, intelligent and hardworking collaborators who nonetheless could never produce anything sustainable because the mission got bogged down in a lack of political will, where plans were drafted and implemented within the framework of one-year mandates. MONUSCO had become a huge structure with too little coordination between its different elements, living in a bubble with its own jargon and trench wars between agencies and departments that mainly wanted to prove how important they were and whose desire for quick success and visibility were at odds with the need for local ownership of solutions. From the beginning, MONUSCO and Congo had been very different planets, and the gaps between the two were widened by the mission's security routines and intervention rituals.[22] In the best case, the Congolese considered the peacekeepers as arrogant and preachy but irrelevant, in the worst case as an accessory to the Great Conspiracy against Congo, motivated only by huge salaries and cheap sex.

This also changed as part of the Framework Agreement, the replacement of Roger Meece by the German diplomat Martin Kobler making a big difference. Kobler had served as the German ambassador to Iraq and Egypt, as chief of cabinet to former German foreign minister Joschka Fischer, and had worked in the Balkans and Palestine. Kobler made a big effort to be closer to the field and communicate with the Congolese population. In addition, there was new leadership on the military side of the mission: new force commander Lieutenant-General Carlos dos Santos Cruz from Brazil and Brigadier-General James Mwakibolwa, the Tanzanian head of the FIB, had joined the mission in June. Both officers were more proactive than their predecessors. But the main reason for MONUSCO's transformation was the fact that the FIB had the mandate to neutralize armed groups responsible for destabilizing the DRC, by carrying out targeted offensive operations, including the use of deadly force, against 'hostile forces' or armed groups.

The simultaneous changes within the FARDC and MONUSCO, including the deployment of the FIB, set the stage for M23's grand finale. By the end of August, M23 had lost territory, troops and morale as a result of fighting with FARDC, the FIB and armed groups in Rutshuru. Between 22 and 24 August, the FIB artillery and attack helicopters backed FARDC ground troops in intense fighting in the Kibati area. Between 24 and 27 August, fighting subsided. M23 suffered losses in terms of both equipment and leadership, with at least seventeen officers killed during this period.

The end of M23 came quickly after the collapse of the negotiations held in Kampala on 21 October. During the lull in fighting between early September and late October, all parties reinforced their positions and prepared for the final battle. On 28 October 2013, FARDC advanced rapidly and pushed M23 back to its strongholds close to the border with Uganda and Rwanda. In early November, some M23 combatants surrendered in Congo and others retreated to Rwanda. On 5 November the bulk of the remaining troops crossed the Ugandan border, commanded by General Sultani Makenga.

An important reason for M23's decline was the fact that Rwanda faced a much more critical attitude from its most loyal international partners than in the past. The concrete consequence was that, in stark contrast with the M23 offensive a year earlier, M23 officers did not manage to get through to their Rwandan counterparts. Several M23 leaders confirmed that when they rang the phone was simply not answered.

The M23 crisis had shaken Congo to its foundations. The uprising had taken eighteen months, but many actors came out of it weakened, and Congo had, once more, been brought close to implosion. Rwanda also came out badly, losing the support of its partners and the privileged position it occupied in eastern Congo after *Umoja Wetu*. The crisis had been the direct result of *Umoja Wetu*'s bankruptcy, the superficial integration of CNDP into the FARDC, which alienated the people even further from the army, and the deep unrest and unresolved trauma the replacement of Nkunda by Ntaganda had caused in the Congolese Tutsi community. In addition, the M23 misadventure was the consequence of decades-long insufficient political will to address the root causes of the conflict.

The people of Kivu welcomed what they considered as very much a military victory by the FARDC. Which it was, although of course a long process of decision-making on different levels had led to that victory. In any case it had an immediate impact on the relationship between the population and the army. I took the opportunity after the end of the war to travel extensively in Kivu, back and forth overland from Kampala to Bukavu, and I found it remarkable how fast the atmosphere had changed. In November and December 2013, a timid trust and pride was tangible in the way the population regarded the armed forces. People felt proud of their army and felt protected by it. There was less fear. This was new. In Virunga National Park I talked to the commander of a small army camp overlooking the border with Uganda, who told me: 'Everything has changed now, and people are happy when they see us. But it is all so fragile. M23 has not been dismantled. Someone can reorganize and arm them any time. It is not over.'

Nothing particularly spectacular took place immediately after the military victory, unless you consider Kabila's improvised tour to the east a major event. On 20 November, he flew with a big group of ministers, collaborators and other officials to Kisangani. In the weeks following, he travelled with his entourage in a huge convoy overland from Kisangani through Beni and Butembo to Goma and later to Bukavu, most of the time driving himself.

The Kampala talks came to an end, not in the Ugandan capital but in Nairobi. On 12 December, the Congolese government and M23 concluded their talks with something that was not quite accurately called a 'peace agreement'. No single document carried both parties' signature. The Congolese government and M23 each made their own statement which were both covered by an overall declaration signed by President Museveni as chair of ICGLR and President Banda as chair of SADC. The 'agreement' thus consists of three separate documents, with M23's commitment to end the rebellion and become a political party, a partial amnesty for M23 members (only for common acts of war or insurgency, not for criminal behaviour in terms of international law, war crimes or crimes against humanity) and the demobilization of former M23 members.

Three developments were important in consolidating the window of opportunity created by the end of the violence: Congo's progress in the reforms the government committed itself to in Addis

Ababa, the neutralization of other armed groups after the disappearance of M23 from the scene, and convincing steps forward in the construction of a truly national, disciplined and efficient army. Without clear results in these fields, there would be a risk that M23 would bounce back in one way or another, especially as the defeated army had only partially been dismantled. Bits of it had sought and found refuge across the border in Rwanda and Uganda.

A lot would depend on the implementation of the 'homework' the Congolese government had committed itself to by signing the PSCF Agreement. This included reforming the security sector and government institutions, consolidating state authority in the east and preventing armed groups from destabilizing neighbouring countries, and strengthening the agenda of reconciliation, tolerance and democratization in order to make progress in the decentralization process.

The PSCF Agreement and the Terms of Reference of the FIB stipulated also that not only M23 but also the other armed groups had to be disarmed. Rwanda required action against FDLR as soon as possible after M23 left Kivu. When talking to people in the field in November and December 2013, I did not get the impression that they were close to launching military action against the Hutu rebels. My contacts in the army were not preparing a campaign and my friends within Congolese civil society who monitored FDLR movements did not observe signs of FDLR units being nervous or under pressure. This was, among other reasons, because of the high risk of collateral damage in a landscape with many 'grey zones' between FDLR fighters, Rwandan Hutu civilians, Congolese Hutu militia men and Congolese Hutu civilians. Preparations for the next military campaign were, rather, focusing on ADF-Nalu, because of the alleged Islamist agenda of this militia with Ugandan roots – one of the oldest but least understood armed groups in the Kivus. Around Christmas 2013, ADF-Nalu tried to reinforce its positions around Watalinga, which eventually led to the killing of at least forty civilians in Kamango, near the Ugandan border.

Whilst the end of the road undoubtedly remained distant, at least the armed forces had made progress and won their first major victory since time immemorial. Perhaps this event carries the seeds of the Congolese state's full renaissance. Two people in particular were identified with the victory in Kivutian public opinion: General Lucien Bahuma, who replaced Mayala Vainqueur as army chief in North Kivu, and the flamboyant young Colonel Mamadou Ndala. The latter's troops were on the frontline, fighting M23 rebels, and he stood with his men at the front. He had the reputation of instilling discipline in his soldiers, with any infraction being met by swift punishment. His unit was not feared by civilians, but respected and loved. After M23 had disappeared from Kivu, Colonel Mamadou became an icon. When rumours started to spread that Kabila would reallocate Mamadou elsewhere in Congo, demonstrations were held in Goma and other cities in the province. In the end, he remained in North Kivu and was deployed as commander of the operations against ADF-Nalu.

On 2 January 2014, however, Colonel Mamadou was killed in an ambush near Beni. The initial hypothesis was that ADF-Nalu was responsible for his death, but it could not be ruled out that he was killed by a hit-and-run action carried out by M23.

A subsequent investigation, though, revealed that Mamadou was killed by FARDC officers who felt threatened by the young colonel's rising star, and the consequences that could have on their own careers and their prospects of earning money from the military campaigns. Despite recent progress in FARDC's performance, the Congolese army remains the product of the slow integration of heterogeneous, undisciplined, badly trained militias whose leadership sometimes has different political affinities, competing ambitions or conflicting business interests. Colonel Mamadou achieved in a very short time a degree of popularity within the community that was previously unheard of. Without doubt, his rise to fame thwarted other people's plans and interests.

It had been heartening travelling in North Kivu in November and December 2013. Of course I knew how fragile it all was, but at least I had travelled in Kivu's tracks with people who had the feeling that, for the first time in two decades, things could change in eastern Congo. That life could return to normality. Change starts in the heads of the people who believe it is possible. The final phase of the M23 crisis had brought the people and the army closer together, and Colonel Mamadou Ndala symbolized that.

His assassination increased the distrust and hostility between different sections of the army. Congo's ability to implement an efficient DDR programme and thus dismantle the remaining armed groups depended on its new-found efficiency and relative transparency, at least in North Kivu. The war had been won because people were paid and the connection between logistics and the military remained tight, with uniforms, arms and ammunition available where and when they were needed. The illusion that the process of change within the FARDC in North Kivu in the second half of 2013 would develop into sustainable steps forward in Congo's security sector reforms sadly disappeared with Colonel Mamadou on 2 January 2014.[23]

Window of opportunity shattered

The fall of Goma had mobilized neighbouring countries, much of the rest of the continent and the wider international community around Congo in a way not seen since the 2006 elections. The military victory had given the Congolese state a renewed confidence, and for the first time Rwanda's partners wanted to keep Rwanda out of Congo. The turn of the year 2013–2014 contained promise of sustainable change. But it soon became clear this was not to be fulfilled.

The PSCF did not only foresee the defeat of M23; the ultimate aim was to dismantle all armed groups in eastern Congo. There was a lot of pressure on Congo to move forward in the struggle against the FDLR. On 30 December 2013, the FDLR declared that it wanted to lay down its arms and continue its fight on a purely political front. On 18 April 2014, they invited international and national actors (and the media) for a disarmament ceremony near Lubero in North Kivu on 30 May. The FDLR did not see this initiative as a surrender, but rather as a unilateral peace deal where it would deliver its weapons and demobilize under the condition of being granted amnesty and the right to start political activities in Rwanda. The DRC government considered this demarche as a positive development that deserved time and space to be implemented. The plan was to disarm the militiamen who surrendered, then bring them to Kisangani to offer them the choice between returning to Rwanda after a proper DDRRR procedure or temporary reallocation in Congo until a permanent location could be found. For obvious reasons, the Congo government preferred a permanent settlement outside its borders.

The government of Rwanda was not convinced that the FDLR's proposal was inspired by a genuine desire to stop its armed struggle, but was instead a cunning plan to avoid an almost certain defeat by the FARDC and the FIB. For Rwanda, the political return of the FDLR was unthinkable and it only wanted to accept individual disarmed FDLR combatants who passed through DDRRR. More than 7,000 former FDLR members had already done this since 2007.

On 30 May, 103 combatants surrendered in North Kivu. Eighty-three others did the same on 9 June in South Kivu. In the months after that, they were joined by a few hundred family members and other dependants, but no new combatants. The FDLR neutralization process was high on the agenda of a joint summit of ICGLR and SADC in early July, where it was decided that the FDLR should be granted six months for its voluntary demobilization. When that deadline passed without further FDLR demobilization a FARDC operation was launched in a climate of tensions between Kinshasa and the UN. But by the end of 2015, it was estimated that FDLR still had between 1,500 and 2,500 troops on the ground, making it by far the largest and most dangerous armed group in eastern Congo, with a chain of command and hierarchy not affected by the operations or the demobilization.[24]

As of early January 2014, the priority for military action against armed groups was given to ADF-Nalu, which occupied the border area between Uganda and Congo. ADF-Nalu had always been the least documented major armed group for various reasons. The rebel group had been founded in 1995 to fight Ugandan President Museveni and gradually took on an Islamic profile. ADF-Nalu is allegedly integrated into a larger jihadist network and wants to create an Islamic state, but there is not much concrete evidence for this. Over the years, the militia absorbed more and more local citizens. By 2014, it was estimated that at least a third of its members were Congolese. Attempts at neutralizing ADF-Nalu in 2005 and in 2010 had been unsuccessful. The group had a number of long periods without military activity, instead focusing on its economic activities and extensive networks, but in 2013 it became increasingly active, expanding kidnapping campaigns, attacking schools, UN peacekeepers and large towns.[25]

On 17 January 2014, the Congolese military began conducting military operations in north-eastern Beni territory, in North Kivu province, against ADF-Nalu. The operations were successful and for months the militia members were dispersed, with 90% of their settlements destroyed. But the military campaign lost its impetus when the commander-in-chief for North Kivu, General Lucien Bahuma, died in unclear circumstances in Uganda.[26] By the end of the year, ADF-Nalu started a very violent campaign against civilians in the area around Beni. In total, ADF combatants attacked thirty-five villages, killing at least 237 civilians between 1 October and 31 December 2014, with several cases of looting and destruction of property also documented. The attackers used machetes, hammers and knives, among other weapons, to wound or execute civilians. Some had their throats slit; others were shot while trying to flee or were burned alive in their homes. These attacks had been carried out by very small units, because the troops had been dispersed by the military campaigns earlier in the year. A UN report[27] stated that the ADF committed the violations, which were systematic and extremely brutal, and which may amount to war crimes and crimes against humanity. It is highly complex to identify the motivations behind the different acts of violence. It is very likely that, in some cases, under the cover of an ADF revenge attack, a different battle was being waged for the economic empire that ADF had established. For part of the violence, the attacks were driven by local politicians to obtain a more strategic position on the local chessboard, with the violence creating opportunities for individuals who, though they may not be behind the attacks, are able to channel popular responses to it in order to shift the local balance of power.[28]

In 2015, ADF-Nalu remained a key player in the massacres around Beni, probably the worst violence in the country that year. Its combatants had been reduced to under 300[29] and its commander Jamil Mukulu was arrested in Tanzania in late April 2015. However, it remained extremely difficult to control the violence, because it was committed by very small and mobile units, and because it was so embedded in local dynamics.

The PSCF had created a new situation in Central Africa but the partnership between the government, the regions and the wider international community quickly disintegrated, not only because of the lack of progress in the neutralization of the armed groups, but also because the implementation of the reforms the Congolese government committed itself to in the Framework Agreement were reduced to a spider's web of formalities, with both a regional and a Congolese follow-up mechanism getting lost in an endless series of technical matrixes and benchmarking exercises, while very little was actually accomplished.[30]

MONUSCO boss Kobler's relationship with the Congolese authorities had started to sour from 2014. The government was upset by the roundtables he initiated with the Congolese opposition and expelled his human rights chief Scott Campbell for reporting abuse by the Congolese security forces. In early 2015, the Congolese government unilaterally announced military operations against the FDLR, despite months of joint planning with MONUSCO. Soon after that, Kabila appointed the commanders of these operations: Generals Fall Sikabwe and Bruno Mandevu, both of whom were blacklisted by the UN for human rights abuses. MONUSCO was side-lined as a result, and lost the credibility it had only recently built up with the successful campaign against M23.[31]

Kobler also lost the confidence of many people within the mission who felt that his search for personal visibility resembled a personality cult. He designed a rather unconvincing project around the creation of 'islands of stability' where the results, if any, would only have a short-term impact. The approach was questioned by Congolese and international observers, with academic researcher Christoph Vogel wondering whether Congo was heading towards 'islands of stability or swamps of insecurity',[32] but the entire civilian section of the mission was mobilized to implement the islands. By doing this, the mission lost a lot of the momentum it had created in 2013.

In 2015, MONUSCO lost most of its political and military leadership, including Special Representative Martin Kobler, its two Deputy Special Representatives of the Secretary-General (SRSGs) Abdallah Wafy and Moustapha Soumaré, and its Force Commander Dos Santos Cruz. They left behind a weakened mission, still the biggest peacekeeping force in the world but not really on speaking terms with the Congolese authorities and deeply distrusted by the population, which is very aware of the astronomic costs of the mission[33] and believes that the output is way below what could be expected for the money. This, and the departure of US Special Envoy for the Great Lakes Region Russ Feingold diminished the capacity of the international community to speak with a single voice.

The PSCF Agreement was an important step in the process towards African ownership of the conflicts and the FIB was a decisive instrument to materialize that. But the issue polarized the climate between countries and regions, with not only political, but also economic interests tangible in the background. The tensions were not only between SADC, ICGLR and East African Community (EAC) countries, but also existed within these structures, between individual countries.

These were interesting developments, and the African institutions' efforts had a remarkable ambiguity. Diplomatic initiatives were launched to prevent the fighting in Congo spilling over to other countries and becoming a regional conflict. At the same time, not much was done to solve the internal Congolese problem. The root causes of the conflicts were not addressed, apart from their being listed in the PSCF Agreement, which was very soon to be considered as just another agreement between people who lacked the commitment to carry out what they had signed up to.

Chapter 7

TOWARDS NEW ELECTIONS OR NEW VIOLENCE?

Kabila's problem with Katanga

Kamerhe's resignation early in 2009 gave an insight into the internal divisions within the president's entourage. Kivu lost influence and Kabila's inner circle became narrower and more Katangese, with Katumba Mwanke and John Numbi in leading roles, and a lot of weight given to people from Maniema, home province of Kabila's mother. But the intra-Katangese tensions inside the regime were polarizing too, reflecting the difficult relations between North and South Katanga.

On the morning of 31 December 2013, less than two months after the defeat of M23, Kinshasa was shaken by three short but violent incidents: lightly armed people entered the building of the RTNC (*Radio et Télévision Nationale Congolaise*), with similar attacks taking place around the military camp Tshatshi and at Ndjili International Airport. Although the confusion of people fleeing and rumours circulating lasted for hours, the police were able to control the situation quite quickly. Later that day there were skirmishes and riots in Lubumbashi, Kindu and Kisangani. On New Year's Eve, the government declared that more than a hundred people had died in the incidents.[1]

The attackers were eventually identified as followers of a religious leader claiming to be the 'Prophet of the Eternal', Paul Joseph Mukungubila. This self-declared prophet lived in Lubumbashi and was a former, if rather unsuccessful, presidential candidate (59,228 votes in 2006) whose heavenly messages were mixed with anti-Kabila and anti-Tutsi hate speech. Mukungubila was a member of the Balubakat community, as was Kabila himself.

The incident happened only two days after the official confirmation of Charles Bisengimana as chief of the national police. Bisengimana, a Tutsi who was part of the rebellion against Laurent Kabila in 1996–1997, had been acting chief since General John Numbi's suspension in June 2010. Until his suspension, Numbi was one of the key personalities of the regime and was still hoping for official rehabilitation. Earlier in 2013, two senior Balubakat leaders had left public life at the highest level. In May 2013, Jean-Claude Masangu had finished his last mandate as president of the Congolese Central Bank. He was replaced by Deo Gratias Mutombo, a technocrat from Katanga, but non-Mulubakat. In addition, Daniel Mulunda Ngoy had to leave the presidency of the CENI in June 2013 because he was held responsible for the loss of legitimacy and stability of the regime in the contested elections of November 2011. He was replaced by the Catholic priest Apollinaire Malumalu, who previously led the commission which had organized the historic elections in 2006.

The actions of Mukungubila's followers were a clear signal that Kabila's own community could no longer be reassured that Kabila was serving its interests well. It was not a coup attempt, as was suggested by several media outlets. And of course the three Balubakat leaders were side-lined only a year after the death of Katumba Mwanke, the key figure in the presidency. Katumba was part of a smaller community from South Katanga. Not only the Balubakat but the entire province feared it was losing its influence.

For many years, tensions have been palpable within the Katangese circles surrounding President Kabila. Katanga is not only the economic heart of Congo – producing the bulk of the central government's tax revenue – it is also the stronghold of the Kabila regime. The government in charge since April 2012 – when the

Mukungubila incident happened – was led by Prime Minister Augustin Matata Ponyo (himself from Maniema), and consisted of two deputy prime ministers, twenty-five ministers and eleven vice-ministers. One deputy prime minister and eight ministers were from Katanga.

Katanga is wealthy but wealth is not evenly distributed. The north of the province, where the Balubakat come from, has been largely absent from the growth dynamics observable in the major cities in the south. The people there blame their own leaders for this: Balubakat leaders have been well-positioned since Laurent-Désiré Kabila took power. While they enriched themselves very visibly, there has been hardly any return for North Katanga. Most politicians in Congolese history have used their mandate to develop their region by improving roads, building schools and hospitals. The population of northern Katanga, and especially the Balubakat community, accuse its leaders of neglecting their own people.

The most violent manifestation of Balubakat discontent at grassroots level is the existence of an armed group known as 'Bakata Katanga' headed by the Mai Mai leader Gédéon Kyungu Mutanga. They have been responsible for massive human rights violations in what is known as the 'Triangle of Death' – the area between Pweto, Manono and Mitwaba where they destroyed villages and symbols of the Congolese state, resulting in the displacement of hundreds of thousands of individuals.

The armed group is rooted in the secessionist history of the province. Bakata Katanga means 'Cutters of Katanga'. Congo had its first implosion less than two weeks after independence, when the Katangan governor Moïse Tshombe unilaterally declared the independence of his province on 11 July 1960 – inspired and supported by Western industrial interest groups. The Congolese government and army were able to reunite the country three years later with the help of UN troops. Since then, the secessionist undercurrent has remained present in the heart of many Katangese from all social strata of the province.

The Bakata Katanga are fed from below by the anger and feelings of exclusion from rural communities. But rather than being a spontaneous outburst of frustration, the movement is believed to be a construction, initiated by people around Kabila.

There had previously been Mai Mai activities in North Katanga as a form of popular resistance against the occupation of eastern Congo by Rwandan troops. Many sources have confirmed that in the period leading up to the 2011 elections, Balubakat in Kabila's inner circle took the initiative in reorganizing the remaining Mai Mai groups under a new operational structure.

Gédéon, one of the leaders of the first wave of Mai Mai groups in North Katanga, was placed in prison and sentenced to death for crimes against humanity during the war. In September 2011, he escaped to take the leadership of the Bakata Katanga. There are many rumours that John Numbi and Jean-Claude Masangu were the people who created Bakata Katanga as a fall-back plan in case Kabila lost the elections against Tshisekedi, but it is very difficult to obtain hard evidence for that.

The development of Bakata Katanga is in many aspects comparable to what happened with other armed groups in Kivu: it can exist because the people in the villages are frustrated and do not feel protected by the state; provincial and national politicians try to steer it but lose their grip after a while because the armed group starts to interact with local dynamics and escapes all forms of control. This includes the control of its own commanders: at the time of writing, Bakata Katanga cannot be considered a coherent organization with a structure, a strategy and a plan but is an amalgam of armed cores without clear lines of command.[2]

On 23 March 2013, a group of Bakata Katanga fighters, many of them women and children armed with machetes and bows and arrows and covered with charms and amulets, marched to Lubumbashi and raised the old flag of independent Katanga in the city's main square. After a battle with security forces that killed thirty-five people, the militants forced their way into a UN compound where 245 of them surrendered.

After this incident, the military operations of the Congolese army against Bakata Katanga intensified and managed to considerably weaken the armed group. This does not necessarily mean that the security situation improved: the operations dispersed Bakata Katanga in the Triangle of Death, driving them further south in the direction of Lubumbashi and the Kundelungu and Upemba national parks. The pressure on Lubumbashi increased and fears of a rebel attack on the city ran rampant.

The most sensitive issue in the intra-Katanga tensions was the pending decentralization, particularly one dimension of it: the *découpage* – the splitting of the existing eleven provinces into twenty-six smaller ones – is foreseen in the constitution. This new territorial structure will be problematic in many places in Congo, because new balances will have to be sought, not only in terms of identity and ethnicity, but also regarding economic interests.[3]

The Katanga case is particularly sensitive. Splitting Katanga into the four new provinces of Haut-Katanga, Haut-Lomami, Tanganika and Luluaba will exacerbate divisions between richer and economically unviable parts of Katanga. The mining history of the province led to complex patterns within the province and from elsewhere, for instance neighbouring Kasai. This has caused tensions and waves of violence in the past between communities, along ethnic lines but with socioeconomic root causes.

Balubakat, in control of lucrative economic activities (mining, transport, trade) in Lubumbashi or Kinshasa, would be reduced to foreigners in the south of Katanga and cut off from an important part of their profits. The *découpage* of Katanga was potentially explosive and there was a lot of pressure from the local business community to avoid its implementation.

The tensions between North and South Katanga increased in the circles of power around Kabila in Kinshasa, but in Katanga itself they have remained mostly under the surface since Moïse Katumbi became governor of the province in March 2007. He has managed to mobilize a lot of support, introducing a new dynamic in the provincial capital of Lubumbashi and in other parts of the province. His charisma seems to work far beyond the borders of his own community (on his mother's side, he is a Bemba from South Katanga) and his region.

Will he stay or will he go?

After the defeat of M23 in November 2013, the political process returned to the forefront in the DRC. A few weeks earlier, Kabila had organized the *Concertations Nationales* that he had announced after M23 left Goma in December 2012.

The *Concertations Nationales* lasted for weeks, producing a substantial list of recommendations. A broad government of national unity was announced, with some ministers and civil society members on board, to replace the technocratic government Matata had led since April 2012. But most significant of all, it divided the opposition into two camps. The speaker of the Senate Léon Kengo wa Dondo, co-chair of the *Concertations*, founded a coalition of opposition parties under the name *Opposition Républicaine*, considered by all players and observers as loyal to the regime. Kengo represented the coalition in the follow-up to the *Concertations* and in the negotiations on the formation of the government of national unity. A more radical opposition clustered around Vital Kamerhe, which considered the *Concertations* to be a congress of the existing presidential majority. For them, the *Opposition Républicaine* was just a part of the majority, as they believed Kengo and his allies would ultimately accept any government strategy for the elections, as long as they could be part of it.

In early 2014, Congo tumbled into electoral fever, two-and-a-half years before the elections were supposed to take place. According to the constitution, the country had to have elections before the end of 2016 and President Kabila could not stand for a third term, leaving him with three options: (a) leave office; (b) seek a new mandate; or (c) stay on under his current mandate.

In April 2014, it was obvious that the key players of the Congolese regime were very nervous. There was absolutely no indication how President Kabila was weighing up the different options regarding the end of his constitutional mandate. No one within the inner circle had the impression a successor was waiting in the wings but, on the other hand, Kabila had not given any signal that he wanted to extend his reign beyond its constitutional limits.

In the months that followed, there was a lot of fascinating 'kite flying' from politicians and other public personalities through the media. The idea was to gauge how local and international public opinion would react to the idea of a revision of the current constitution or a referendum on an entirely new one. None of the proposals launched were openly supported by Kabila himself, but it was hard to imagine those colourful kites were flying without his approval.

The pro-revision camp gained confidence and observers expected an apotheosis around the opening of the parliamentary session in mid-September 2014, in the form of the installation of a government of national unity and a smooth passage of the revision through the parliament. But that didn't happen. The regime failed to mobilize the necessary parliamentary majority, and Kabila held Minaku, as the speaker of Parliament, responsible for that failure.

The fact that the regime did not manage to form a government of national unity obviously frustrated the leaders of the *Opposition Républicaine*, and its leader Kengo wa Dondo said in his speech at the opening of the parliamentary session that he was against the revision of the constitution. This was a major blow for the pro-revision camp: the loyal opposition had put its loyalty on hold.

On top of this, significant cracks appeared on the surface of the majority itself. The MSR, the second biggest parliamentary faction within the majority, also declared itself against the revision of the constitution. The MSR and its president Pierre Lumbi were publicly criticized in a meeting of the majority in Kingakati in early October, but its members received silent applause and the encouragement of other parties and individuals within the majority, including from

Kabila's own PPRD. Important players in forming public opinion, such as the Catholic Church and civil society, reinforced their earlier positions against attempts to keep Kabila in power with a new mandate.

Eventually, the government of national unity was installed on 8 December 2014. Kabila's difficulties in finding the necessary regional and political balance for the new government had become a major sign of his vulnerability and led to endless speculation. One of the major obstacles was the question of who would lead it. The more difficult it proved to replace Prime Minister Matata Ponyo, the greater the chances grew that he would remain in post. In the end, he remained prime minister, though in a weaker position than before, having lost much of his direct control over the finances. The 'national unity' of the new government was based on the fact that ministerial responsibilities were given to ten people from the opposition. This time, the political heavyweights were on board: several party leaders became ministers.

The installation of the government of national unity was an important development in favour of the government, creating the impression that Kabila's camp had the ball in its court again. However, this did not last long. On 23 December 2014, the governor Moïse Katumbi returned to Katanga after nearly two months abroad for medical care. Katumbi has a good reputation as a businessman and manager, and is known to be generous. Furthermore, he has the money and looks for a strong campaign, and a charismatic personality. He cunningly uses his success in football (he owns the Tout Puissant Mazembe team of Lubumbashi) and development to feed into his political ambitions. Katumbi was seen as one of the few politicians, perhaps the only one, able to mobilize a considerable electorate in most of the provinces. He was welcomed back by an enthusiastic crowd of people, and for the first time he spoke out against Kabila remaining in power beyond 2016.

In January 2015,[5] the government attempted to pass a law that would integrate a population census into the electoral calendar.

While a census would be welcome in principle, the timing was seen as an attempt to slow down the electoral process, extending Kabila's current mandate by at least two years. After days of protests, the government was forced to withdraw the law. Again, the initiative to sink it was taken by Kengo wa Dondo.

In March 2015, critical voices within the ruling majority crystallized in the members of G7, a group which some see as a coalition of the moderate and which others view as simply *les frondeurs* ('the troublemakers').

The group finds its origins in the dissidence of Pierre Lumbi, president of the MSR party, when he spoke out against the proposed constitutional change in September 2014. Lumbi was later joined by six other disillusioned figures, amongst whom were Planning Minister Olivier Kamitatu (ARC) and three leaders from Katanga, including *'baba ya Katanga'* (father of Katanga) Kyungu wa Kumanza.[6] Together they form an interesting mix of regions, generations, social backgrounds and skills.[7]

In March, the G7 published its first open letter to Kabila in which the group asked the president to communicate his plans clearly. They also expressed concerns about the local elections and the policy of *découpage* by which the DRC's eleven provinces were to be split into twenty-six provinces. The G7 figures were hugely anxious at the havoc the president might cause in the country if he attempted to maintain his grip on power.

For Kabila, the G7 was too big to be ignored yet too small to make much difference. Together, the seven parties represented by the group's leaders had seventy-nine seats in parliament, yet the entire majority (including that seventy-nine) held 353 seats out of a total 500.

The seven party leaders themselves hesitated as to whether to remain within the majority to encourage internal debate or to become a broader movement, potentially joining forces with opposition parties. In the end, Kabila's decision to throw them out of the ruling majority, after their second letter in September, made the choice for them.

When talking to the different personalities within the G7, one does not get the impression that any of the party leaders saw himself as the DRC's next president. Pierre Lumbi, for instance, told me: 'People like myself will have to be satisfied with a post of ambassador, because we cannot incarnate the cry for change at the highest level.'[8] Rather, it seemed likely that the group would work together with Moïse Katumbi, the figure seen as the clearest challenger to Kabila.

Meanwhile, Kabila remained silent about his future intentions, and this weighed heavily on the entire regime. Though Kabila had a strong team around him in the early years of his presidency, in more recent years he has tended to meet with key leaders individually and give them orders of which the others were not aware. A holistic approach disappeared and no minister dared take a decision without approval from Kabila's cabinet. As a result, there was a lot of bitterness and competition in the regime.

People could win and lose support very fast. In early 2014 for instance, the speaker of Parliament Aubin Minaku seemed in a good position to be Kabila's anointed successor. But within less than a year he disappointed the president on three occasions: he failed to mobilize the parliamentary majority necessary to change the constitution; he was unable to organize the follow-up to the national consultations; and he was incapable of stemming dissidence within the ruling party as the G7 emerged.

When Kabila eventually installed the government of national unity in December 2014, a different figure was elevated to prominence. After the 2011 elections, Evariste Boshab, at that time speaker of Parliament and the most influential apparatchik of PPRD, considered himself the obvious next prime minister, and was therefore not amused when he was left out of Prime Minister Augustin Matata's technocratic government. However, he came back into favour in December 2014 as vice-prime minister and minister of the interior and security. Boshab openly supported a revision of the constitution in favour of a third mandate for Kabila and organized the repression of demonstrators who protested in January 2015 against the electoral law, in which at least forty people were killed. Afterwards, however, Boshab lost influence with Kabila, who is understood to have held the vice-PM responsible for the failure to pass the electoral law, and in May 2015 Boshab was replaced by Henri Mova as secretary-general of the PPRD.

Another emerging personality in the regime was Kalev Mutondo, chief of the *Agence National des Renseignements* (ANR). He increased in prominence as he became Kabila's main messenger to the opposition in laying the groundwork for a national dialogue. Kabila's inner circle wanted to organize this national dialogue in September 2015, in order to conclude it was no longer possible to organize timely elections and to install a new government of national unity , with a key role for the UDPS. This new government, according to the plan, would oversee a three-year transition period up to the end of 2018. In this time, the constitution would be revised, provincial and senate elections would be held in 2016, and local elections would be conducted in 2017. Presidential elections would then finally be held in 2018. In this scenario, Kabila would not only remain president during the transition, but would seek election for his first mandate under the Fourth Republic. One of the cornerstones of the scheme was to integrate the UDPS into a new government, but after the opposition party withdrew from the preparatory talks, the dialogue, as well as its architect Kalev Mutondo, lost authority.

The relations between the quartet of Minaku, Boshab, Matata and Mutondo were notoriously bad, and confrontations between them found their way onto the front pages of the capital's newspapers. All of them considered themselves in the race to be Kabila's appointed successor – if he needed one.

In the first weeks of 2015, something significant happened. In Kinshasa and some of the provincial capitals, particularly in Goma, the reaction to the electoral law as it was submitted to the Parliament was very emotional and violent. Human Rights Watch confirmed that thirty-six people, including one police officer, were killed during demonstrations in Kinshasa. Among these, Congo's security forces fatally shot at least twenty-one people. Additionally, on 22 January at least four people were killed during demonstrations in Goma.[9]

Particularly notable was the fact that the demonstrating crowd was only partially following the watchwords of the opposition. Crowds gathered spontaneously, not at places and times set by the opposition. The population does not believe that its daily living conditions or its long-term prospects have considerably improved in the Third Republic, causing great frustration and anger. But the experience in January 2015 taught us that the Congolese population is not only against the continuation of the present regime, it is disconnected from the entire political caste. Politicians are seen as people who try to obtain mandates in order to strengthen and enrich themselves, their family, their clan, their community, and there is not much distinction made between the ruling parties and the opposition.[10]

Congo's political elite know that they lack moral authority over the population as well as the capacity to steer any form of uprising. Furthermore, they know there is something unpredictable and volatile in the people's reactions. The public resistance to a revision of the constitution and a third mandate for Kabila was one of the most important worries for the regime. Civil society has, for many reasons, lost the capacity to mobilize the population and organize big demonstrations or *Actions-ville-morte*, with churches probably the only source of credible leadership accepted by a large part of the population, but even here the churches are divided amongst themselves.

In the recent past three political parties have displayed the capacity to mobilize considerable numbers of people for meetings and demonstrations in Kinshasa: PALU, UDPS and to a lesser extent MLC. However, the three parties struggle with the same problem: they live under the shadow of an absent historical leader. Gizenga (PALU) and Tshisekedi (UDPS) are old and ill. There is a lot of rivalry within the parties over the political patrimony of the president. Family ties, regional divisions and/or ideological and strategic disagreements dominate this competition. Bemba's case (MLC) of course is different: he remains in the ICC prison, and retains his aura of a strong leader and a victim of Kabila's dictatorship in the eyes of a considerable part of his electorate. In the meantime, though, his party has split. It is hard to gauge to what extent these three parties have the ability to mobilize the frustrated population of Congo's capital.

Most of my interlocutors during my research in March 2016 did not rule out a spontaneous popular outburst of frustration and anger in Kinshasa or elsewhere in Congo. Directly beneath the surface of their anger they harbour a very violent discourse: 'we live in conditions that exist nowhere else. The man at the top is responsible. His time is running out. But if he stays one day longer than the mandate we gave him, the people will chase him and his regime out'. The frustration and anger of the people was crystallizing around the constitutional limits of Kabila's power. A remarkable majority of the people I spoke with considered violence at this point an inevitable outcome of the political crisis. The trigger might not necessarily be political and could just as well come from the social realm, for instance through demonstrations and riots by socially vulnerable but well-organized groups in society, such as people working at the bottom end of public transport (motorcyclists and drivers of small taxis), vendors of prepaid telephone cards or *shegue*, as street kids are called in Kinshasa. There was a considerable risk that any form of popular uprising could quickly degenerate into blind violence and plundering, thereby causing a lot of human, material and institutional damage, before being quickly suppressed by the security forces.[11]

A new development in the first half of 2015 was the fact that the Congolese authorities started to fear new forms of mobilization initiated by youth movements such as La Lucha in Goma. La Lucha celebrated three years of existence on 1 May 2015. It is a movement of young people who try to put the issue of good governance at the forefront of their actions, encouraging the citizens to question the authorities in terms of: why don't we have water in this town? What happened to the roads you started to construct long ago but never finished? They want to raise awareness within the population about the rights and obligations of all parties involved in a functioning democracy, inviting authorities to say what they do and to do what they say, and to communicate what they plan.

They work in an entirely new spirit. The youth movement likes to state:

> We are not an organization. We don't have the ambition to become one. Even less are we an NGO. We don't need statutes or a board of administrators. We won't try to get officially registered. Our actions cost money but we are not looking for donors. We try to mobilize the necessary funds by scratching the last francs from our pockets.[12]

For this, they use youngsters as a lever. Young people are demographically very important in Congo and might be marginalized in the elections. Together with similar organizations, La Lucha tried to set up a national network under the name *Filimbi* on 15 March 2015 but all its participants were arrested. It remains a small group of people with a narrow social base, but in my own research it became clear that non-intellectual youth groups and organizations of the have-nots were also closely following La Lucha's public statements and the repression deployed against them.

Deconstructing the state to remain in power

The government failed to revise the constitution and change the electoral law in Parliament, and the failed attempts to do so weakened Kabila, exposing his political vulnerability. But different strategies were used to organize the slippage, slowing down the process in order to prevent the elections being held due to constitutional delays. The regime went very far in this, dismantling important state institutions such as the provincial governments and the electoral commission.

Decentralization is a long-running issue in the DRC. The discussion about the balance of power between the central state in the capital and the provincial institutions divided its first genera-tion of politicians, and was the cause of secession wars. The 2006 Constitution of the Third Republic defines Congo as a federal state where the provinces have political, fiscal and juridical autonomy and important responsibilities in the organization of public life, with three significant changes to the pre-existing constitution. First, decentralization would give more resources to the provinces, with each province destined to keep 40% of the revenue it generates internally. Second, within three years, the eleven provinces were to be divided into twenty-six, with existing districts becoming proper provinces. Third, the constitution created a number of elected assemblies; at the national, provincial (i.e. district) and local levels (i.e. *communes, secteurs* and *chefferies*[13]).

On 19 July 2015, eight years after launching the decentralization process with the establishment of provincial assemblies and govern-ments in 2007, the partition of the Congolese territory (from eleven to twenty-six provinces) was completed according to Article 226 of the 2006 Constitution. Evariste Boshab, minister of the interior and security, announced the implementation a few months earlier, in March. He respected the deadline of mid-July 2015 he set himself, although this seemed more the result of improvisation than of the effective, pragmatic and evolutionary approach he had referred to.

The territorial *découpage* creates smaller and decentralized units of governance which are in principle easier to administer. However, several provinces lack adequate administrative infrastructure as well as financial and human resources. The uneven distribution of resources will inevitably trigger conflicts about the redistribution of financial reserves and other resources from the old to the new provincial entities. The lack of sufficient qualified personnel also threatens to hamper genuine decentralized governance.

The implementation of *découpage* is an enormous political and logistical challenge that can only succeed if the government has the will and ability to allocate appropriate resources to the new provinces. If not adequately funded, these new administrative entities will not be fully operational and will be unable to strengthen accountable and democratic governance at the provincial and local level.

The professed aim of decentralization is to reinforce good governance and accountability, improve administrative efficiency and increase the democratic participation of citizens. It is difficult to argue against that, but the decision to implement the decentralization process now increases the difficulties of implementing the electoral calendar in a timely fashion. At this moment, the newly created provinces do not have the personnel, institutions, financial means, infrastructure or logistics to function properly, and the appointment of provisional governors (called 'special commissioners') to organize the provincial elections is an important step towards the central government gaining more control over the provincial institutions. Control of the provincial assemblies is very important for the presidential majority because these assemblies elect the senators. The current Senate, particularly its speaker Kengo wa Dondo, is not controlled by the presidential majority and has in the past prevented the passing of laws proposed by the majority.

Probably the most important reason for the government pressing forward with decentralization was the fact that the process dismantled the province of Katanga and deprived its governor and potential presidential candidate Moïse Katumbi of his political status and identity. It is highly significant that one of the last deeds Katumbi performed as governor was to inaugurate a monument to Katangese identity, together with Kyungu wa Kumanza, the speaker of the provincial assembly and an important leader of northern Katanga.

A second striking example of how the Congolese regime tried to remain in power by boycotting the functioning of its own state is the Independent National Electoral Commission. The CENI published a global calendar on 12 February 2015, listing all the steps in the electoral process, starting with the construction of the CENI's offices and storage, the recruitment of its agents etc., via the organization of provincial and local elections on 25 October 2015, the indirect elections of governors and senators in January 2016 up to the presidential and legislative elections on 27 November 2016 and the swearing in ceremony of the elected president on 20 December 2016. This calendar was considered by most national and international observers as unrealistic, especially as it was expected that the political, administrative and logistic complexity of the local elections (planned since 2006 but never organized) would slow down the electoral process and inevitably carry Kabila's present mandate beyond its constitutional limit.

The issue of integrating people who had turned eighteen since its last review into the electoral register was one of many unsolved questions. From a democratic viewpoint it is hard to imagine elections without this demographically and politically very important part of the population on board, but it costs time and money to register them.

Following CENI's presentation of the global calendar, there was delay upon delay. There were several reasons for this. There was a total lack of ownership by the Congolese government over the process, which could even be considered an active boycott. The necessary and budgeted sums to organize the different steps of the process were systematically not disbursed. There was a constant struggle between the CENI and the government (in the first place Prime Minister Matata and Vice-Prime Minister Boshab) for control over the electoral process. In recent years, the CENI received only 17%[14] of its budgeted running costs to organize the different phases of the electoral process, making it impossible to organize the planned operations.

Secondly, there was absolutely no enthusiasm within the international community to participate financially in an electoral process without clear commitment and ownership on the part of the Congolese government. It was very unlikely that the international community would engage with the process without evidence of the government's goodwill and an effective disbursement scheme. And thirdly, in December 2014, Malumalu was struck by a brain tumour, underwent brain surgery twice and had a cerebral haemorrhage in between. He has spent most of the time since then outside the country, first in South Africa and later in the US. His absence obviously weighed on the work of the commission, even if he tried to chair it as well as he could through video-conferences. Eventually, he resigned on 11 October 2015, and was replaced by Corneille Nangaa, who was involved in the electoral process in 2006. Although many observers agree that Nangaa has the technical skills to lead the complex electoral process, it is unlikely he has Malumalu's organizational capacity and political stature to guarantee the independence of the electoral commission.

CONCLUSION

I first decided to write this book in November 2012, the day after Goma fell. Congo seemed close to a new implosion. I started discussions with Zed Books one year later, November 2013, in the weeks after M23 was defeated. There was a wave of optimism that, maybe, sometime soon, the DRC could become a 'normal country', with effective democratic institutions and an army that protected the population instead of being a source of harassment, rape and pillage. By the time we signed the contract in March 2014, that window of opportunity was already shattered: the army remained what it was; the east remained a breeding ground for conflict and violence; and the Congolese government had not made any progress in implementing the reforms on democracy, governance and human rights to which it had committed itself in the PSCF Agreement. From 2014 onwards, Congo entered a period of electoral fever, focused on the question of whether Kabila would try to stay in power or leave office when his second mandate as elected president of the Third Republic expired on midnight of 19 December 2016.

As I finish writing this book in the very first days of 2017, we know that 2016 was an electoral year without elections. Kabila is still president, and the country's institutions were not swept away by uncontrollable street violence as many people had anticipated.

Some events in early 2016 made it clear how emotionally people may react, how quickly they can come together in large groups, and how fast such gatherings can take on an explicit anti-Kabila character. The Congo national football team's victory in the African Nations Championship in February was just such a moment. After every game, an increasing number of people celebrated the victory in the street. When Congo defeated Mali in the final, victory was celebrated in the streets with a strange cocktail of extreme happiness, due to the victory, and extreme anger, expressed by shouting anti-Kabila slogans and chanting Yebela, a song which means: 'Watch out, everything has a beginning and an end, soon your mandate is over.' I had the bad idea of watching the cup final in a more remote suburb of Kinshasa and it took me hours to drive back to the city centre amidst an excited mass. Those were scary hours.

The regime prepared itself for the possibility of street protests. Surveillance cameras were installed in strategic squares, crossings and streets of the capital. New crowd-and-riot control vehicles and other non-lethal equipment was purchased, while security personnel were being prepared to increase the regime's capacity to anticipate outbursts of violence. There were also many indications that the regime was in the process of recruiting and training young people, organizing them into gangs to intimidate opponents of the regime or infiltrate peaceful gatherings.

I was asked to put together a small research team[1] for a preliminary analysis of how people at the grassroots level regard the uncertainties of the ongoing electoral process, what their view on the process is, and how they see the near future unfolding. We interviewed people in key positions in the political landscape and organized focus group discussions with academic and uneducated youths, martial arts practitioners and other sports clubs, militant priests and Christian activists at grassroots level, youth groups of political parties, official religious authorities, socioeconomic groups, official spokespersons of civil society, spokespersons from PPRD, opposition parties, and so on.

In all these interviews, it was palpable that the people in the communes and neighbourhoods were frustrated and angry about their precarious living conditions. People have difficulties in feeding themselves and their families, while unemployment is endemic, not only for the unskilled, but also for young graduates and intellectuals. Decent housing is hard to find and unaffordable. Good health care and education are inaccessible. Failing of water and electricity services are also a source of great frustration.

Nearly all the people interviewed located the main responsibility for their poverty with the regime. For them, the achievements of the democratization process do not exist, and nothing has fundamentally changed in the way the country is governed since Mobutu died. I often heard: 'We don't only want to change the driver, we want to change the vehicle as well.' For them, credible change would have to introduce good governance.

Beneath the surface, the discourse is very violent. A remarkable majority of the people we spoke with consider violence at this point an inevitable outcome of the current political crisis.

The frustration and anger of the people at the grassroots level in Kinshasa also focused on Swahili-speaking citizens in the capital, allegedly supporters of the regime: 'I am unemployed because I don't speak Swahili' was a common refrain. The international community was also a target of potential violence, with people claiming: 'We suffer because the international community installed and maintained the present regime against the candidates of our choice.'

The cry for change is partially a generational conflict. Young people are demographically very important and fear they may be marginalized in the elections. Since early 2015, Congolese authorities fear new forms of mobilization such as that initiated by La Lucha. When La Lucha attempted to set up a national network under the name of Filimbi in March 2015, all its participants were arrested. Two of them are still in jail, and many militants have been arrested and imprisoned in Goma while protesting against their detention in Kinshasa.

This was an intense period of networking between formal and informal youth organizations, including the youth leagues of the different political parties. Universities seemed to be the ideal place for youth activism, exchange and joint strategic thinking, and the natural environment for networking among young intellectuals. Several of the focus groups with unskilled and unschooled young-sters used the universities as a reference point for mobilization. Some of them had a very violent view of the way events will develop, but when we asked: 'When will you deploy the actions you planned?', they answered: 'We will observe them [university students]. When they go to the streets, we will follow.'

With the end of Kabila's constitutional mandate approaching, things were getting very unpredictable, but I believe the following three scenarios provide an interesting analytical frame.

(1) Best case scenario: consensus over credible elections within credible delays

A decade ago, the DRC went through a similar situation. After the war, the transition was supposed to end in June 2005. But it was only in December 2006 that Kabila was sworn in as the newly elected president. The delays were not the end of the world, and the public largely accepted them for two main reasons. Firstly, because there was a broad political consensus that they were necessary. And secondly because the transition followed a credible process.

To avoid violence, the political scene needs to construct a broad consensus and put in place a process that can realistically lead to free and fair elections within a reasonable timeframe, with the explicit proviso that Kabila will not stand for a third term. And it will have to sell this consensus to public opinion.

(2) Back to the end of Mobutu's days: chaos and crisis

If there is not an agreement akin to the mid-2000s, and Kabila manages to remain in power beyond his mandated term, the crisis could instead resemble the end of Mobutu's reign. Then, in the mid-1990s, any form of process seemed to evaporate to the point that no one knew what to expect. Mobutu manoeuvred the CNS into a hole by creating side procedures and divisions so that nobody had any idea what should happen next or even what to expect.

Signs of a similar trend may already be emerging. The paralysis of CENI and the decentralization of the country in 2015 certainly create the impression of a deliberate deconstruction of the state. Seen through this lens, the situation in January 2017 is not so different from the chaos and uncertainty at the end of Mobutu's reign.

(3) Worst case scenario: state implosion under pressure from the street

A final scenario then is that large-scale violence kicks off in a major city – with Kinshasa, Lubumbashi, Goma and Bukavu seemingly the most likely – which in turn triggers a rapid implosion of the state and the crumbling of its institutions. This would create a highly unpredictable situation as well as one likely to be destructive in human, material and institutional terms. The confrontation between protest and repression could not only easily degenerate into violence, chaos and the annihilation of all the achievements since the official end of the war in 2002, but, as a worst case scenario, could even lead to a situation comparable to Somalia two decades ago.

Many people expected such a wave of violence on 19 December. Yet on that day things remained relatively calm in the country, due to the massive deployment of security forces, which had a dramatic intimidating effect on the people. On 20 December, the first day after Kabila's mandate expired, twenty protesters are reported to have been killed in confrontations with security forces, most of them in Kinshasa and Lubumbashi.

In September 2016, Kabila finally managed to start the dialogue he had announced more than a year earlier. Few across the Kinshasa political spectrum have much faith in the dialogue as currently configured. Lack of clarity over the selection of participants, uncertainty over the agenda and poor public communication are the main concerns. With fewer than 300 participants, the dialogue is not large enough to serve as a forum to air national concerns, but too large for the main actors to strike the necessary deals.[2] Some of the opposition leaders are participating, the most prominent among them being Vital Kamerhe. But other important leaders and their parties remain outside the conference room: Etienne Tshisekedi, Moïse Katumbi, the entire G7 and many more have refused to participate.

An agreement was signed on 18 October 2016 but it was widely considered not inclusive enough, or at least not a broad enough consensus for the country to enter a new transition which has a reasonable chance of free and fair elections in a relatively short period. This lack of confidence did not improve when, one month later, Kabila appointed Samy Badibanga as prime minister of the transitional government. Badibanga was a politician with a UDPS background, born and bred in Kinshasa but with roots in the Kasai. He was elected as MP in 2011, and excluded from the party by Tshise-kedi, who did not want his elected MPs to take up their mandate. By appointing a prime minister who was somewhat isolated on the political chessboard and with no executive experience whatsoever, Kabila made clear that free and fair elections within a reasonable timescale were not his priority.

In December, the Catholic bishops, united in Cenco (*Conférence épiscopale nationale du Congo*), undertook a last démarche to broaden the support for the transition and eventually, on 31 December at 11.45 pm, a new agreement was signed which stated that Kabila would not stand for a third mandate, or try to change the constitution, and elections would be held before the end of 2017. Kabila would remain president during the transition, some-thing which confirmed a High Court decision six months earlier. The court proclaimed Kabila could stay on as long as there was no elected successor.

A lot of pressure made that agreement possible, the two most important players being Cenco itself and SADC, especially Angola. Cenco had been pressurized itself by its own base, the believers, who shared the general feeling within public opinion that it was time for Kabila to go. Angola had been a loyal partner of the regime, saving it on several occasions, but the country no longer believed Kabila could provide enough stability to avoid a new implosion which would without doubt affect Congo's nine neighbouring countries and the wider region.

At the time of writing, the Democratic Republic of Congo has just started another transition, based on a shaky agreement, signed by an internally divided majority and an internally divided opposition, in a country with a sad tradition of agreements signed by people without any genuine commitment to respecting what they have agreed.

In November 2013, after the defeat of M23, hopes were raised that the cycle of violence would come to an end, and that soon afterwards all armed groups would disappear from Kivu. This also did not happen. Today, Christoph Vogel and Jason Stearns estimate that at least seventy armed groups are active in eastern Congo, most of them numbering no more than 200 combatants recruited along ethnic lines. An estimated 1.6 million Congolese civilians remain internally displaced.[3]

The continuation and fragmentation of armed groups is due to the failure of various demobilization, stabilization and security sector reform programmes, which never managed to create economically solid alternatives for demobilized militia members or to address local conflicts and security problems, which continue to find their origin in customary succession and land issues and can be instrumentalized by political elites in the region.[4] The different power-sharing agreements Congo has adopted since the start of the peace process in 1999 have not managed to integrate armed groups and their wider networks into the state institutions, for many reasons, including their own lack of coherence and the fact that the communities they claimed to represent never felt their interests were served by the armed groups at the negotiation table or in the government.[5]

As I write, most of the local conflicts in Kivu are polarizing again. The situation in Beni has been the most dramatic and visible conflict, but the tensions are increasing in different places, including the Ruzizi plains visited in the section about Mutarule, at the end of Chapter 2. The security situation degenerated after the massacre.

General Masunzu was withdrawn as the commander of the military region of South Kivu,[6] and his departure was problematic for his community, the Banyamulenge, which for years considered his leadership over the army in the province as their main protection. New armed groups are forming inside the community. Meanwhile, the failed electoral process in Burundi not only annihilated all the progress the country had made in terms of reconciliation, peace-building and democracy since 2000, it also destabilized Congo, because Kivu is fertile ground for the Burundian armed opposition to flourish. Rwanda facilitates this and is involved in organizing it. The identity and land issues polarize rapidly in the Ruzizi plains, and the potential of trans-border violence is growing as well. The arrival of Burundian refugees has created a humanitarian crisis in the south of South Kivu, with approximately 15,000 refugees so far registered. This has an immediate and negative influence on the ethnic tensions in the territories of Uvira and Fizi, with their delicate inter-ethnic balances. In the plain of the Ruzizi alone, Vogel and Stearns counted fifteen armed groups, including groups based in the Moyen Plateau overlooking the plains.[7]

The south of South Kivu is just one example of how local conflicts and their unresolved root causes can trigger regional violence, with the Congolese state still not rising from its ashes and an international community aware of the meagre impact of its past approaches in the field and its lack of political leverage.

Different incidents in the last months of 2016, mainly but not exclusively in eastern Congo, made clear that the state was no longer able to handle the root causes of the Congolese conflicts: communities polarizing on identity and land issues, and governance deteriorating in a climate of uncertainty as to the immediate political future.[8]

In addition, the chances of trans-border violence and conflict are increasing. Not only did two neighbouring states of Congo implode in recent years (Central African Republic and South Sudan), but the consequences of the failed electoral process in Burundi in 2015 have had a very negative impact on Kivu.

In 2015, the Burundian president Pierre Nkurunziza managed to obtain a third mandate, albeit at a very high cost: all the achievements of the Arusha peace agreement of 2000 were destroyed and a country which effectively had achieved post-conflict status suddenly stands on the brink of another civil war. The Burundian experience, however devastating it may be turn out to be, is a signal to President Kabila that it might pay to hang onto his mandate despite all the pressure. In 2016, the long reigns of Yoweri Museveni (President of Uganda since 1986) and Denis Sassou-Nguesso (President of the Republic of Congo from 1979 to 1992 and then again from 1997 to date) were once more extended, which does not provide much incentive for Kabila to respect his constitution and prepare for departure. Kagame also decided to seek a third mandate as President of Rwanda.

The events in each of these countries will influence the others, especially regarding the possibility of presidents remaining in power beyond what is constitutionally permissible.

Congo remains and will continue to be a roller coaster of events and emotions where one should always expect the unexpected. The peace process and the Third Republic installed institutions which were not very operational but gave some structure to the state. Outside the major cities, however, the state does not have the capability of addressing the old issues of identity and land, and cannot react effectively to the increasing incidents and tensions. The immediate future looks bleak for Congo.

NOTES

Introduction

1 The war in Congo between 1998 and 2002 was immediately called the first African World War or the Great African War, because armies of nine different countries were involved, alongside a huge number of armed groups. The term was contested though, because the war was mainly fought in Congo and only African countries fought on the ground.

2 The International Rescue Committee (IRC) in 2007 published a study claiming that more than 5.4 million people had died there since the start of the war in August 1998. This figure was later contested in other studies.

3 Autesserre, 2012.

4 Prunier, 2009.

5 Autesserre, 2012.

6 Ibid.

Chapter 1

1 Deibert, 2014, p. 18.

2 This French term referred to the Congolese elite who were well on their way to becoming European, because they had adopted western values and patterns of behaviour through education and assimilation.

3 Berwouts, 2001.

4 Ibid.

5 Van Reybrouck, 2014, pp. 282–303.

6 In 1999 Ludo De Witte published a very detailed book about the assassination of Lumumba. In 2001, it was translated into English.

7 Martens, 1985.

8 Van Reybrouck, 2014, p. 341.

9 Ibid., p. 342.

10 Trefon, 2011, p. 19.

11 Deibert, 2014, pp. 31–34.

12 Lemarchand, 2001, pp. 17–19.

13 Vansina, 1982, quoted by Lemarchand, 2001, p. 18.

14 Van Reybrouck, 2014, p. 370.

15   Rotberg, 2003, pp. 37–38.
16   Coolsaet, 2008, pp. 61–62.
17   Reyntjens, 2010.
18   Prunier, 2009, p. 148.
19   United Nations, 2010, para. 522.
20   Guevara, 2000.
21   Kennes, 2003.
22   Prunier, 2009, p. 128.
23   Van Reybrouck, 2014, p. 425.
24   Ibid., p. 426.
25   Prunier, 2009, p149
26   Laurent Kabila was called Mzee, Swahili for old man, a term with a lot of respect.
27   Prunier, 2009, p. 151.
28   Reyntjens, 2010.
29   Prunier, 2009, p. 183.
30   Stearns, 2012b, pp. 188–192.
31   Van Reybrouck, 2014, p. 445.
32   Prunier, 2009.
33   Stearns, 2012b, pp. 219–225.
34   Ibid., pp. 235–237.
35   Prunier, 2009, pp. 173–177.
36   Ibid., pp. 265–277.
37   Ibid., pp. 265–277.
38   *Murder in Kinshasa*, documentary by Arnaud Zajtman produced in 2011.
39   Van Reybrouck, 2014, p. 467ff.
40   Willame, 2007; de Villers, 2009.
41   Van Reybrouck, 2014, pp. 133–134.
42   Ibid.
43   Prunier, 2009.
44   Stearns, 2012b, pp. 285–290.
45   Reyntjens, 2010, p. 206.
46   Interviews with insiders in the Rwandan government and army.
47   Ibid.
48   Reyntjens, 2010, pp. 203–210.
49   Van Reybrouck, 2014, p. 457.

Chapter 2

1   Mathys, 2014.
2   Newbury, 2009, p. 9.
3   Mathys, 2014.

4   Newbury, 2009, pp. 129–141.
5   Mathys, 2014, p. 168.
6   Vlassenroot, 2013.
7   Willame, 1997, p. 40.
8   Bouvy and Lange, 2012, pp. 18–19.
9   Huggins, 2010; Vlassenroot, 2013.
10 Bouvy and Lange, 2012, p. 18.
11 Stearns, 2012a.
12 Huggins, 2010, pp. 15–19.
13 Stearns, 2012a, p. 23.
14 Bouvy and Lange, 2012, pp. 20–21.
15 Stearns, 2012a, pp. 23–27.
16 Bouvy and Lange, 2012, pp. 20–22.
17 Prunier, 1997.
18 Mararo, 1997.
19 International Alert, 2015.[N.19]
20 Most of this part is based on my own research. I was in South Kivu in that period, doing a consultancy for an international NGO specializing in local conflict transformation. A summary was published on African Arguments on 18 June 2014 with the title 'The Mutarule massacre: conflict from below in eastern Congo'.
21 Kyalangalilwa, 2014.
22 Life and Peace Institute, 2012.
23 I refer to communities by using the nominal class system of Bantu languages, which means that, for instance for the Fuliro community, a single member of the community is called a Mufuliro. The plural is Bafuliro.
24 The figures differ.

Chapter 3

1   Prunier, 2009, pp. 300–301.
2   de Villers, 2009, pp. 276–278.
3   Willame, 2007.
4   Trefon, 2011, pp. 22–23.
5   Prunier, 2009, p.296.
6   Deibert, 2014, p. 86.
7   de Villers, 2009, pp. 312–313.
8   Prunier, 2009, p. 309.
9   Enough Project, 2014.
10 Interviews with key people in Kabila's team as well as JMAC (Joint Mission Analysis Centre) staff and members of the UN Group of Experts.
11 In May 2002 soldiers and police officers in Kisangani, the third largest city in

Congo, mutinied against their commanding officers and the local authorities of RCD/Goma. Six RCD personnel were killed. When RCD reinforcements arrived from Goma, soldiers entered the residential district of Mangobo, killing dozens of civilians, committing numerous rapes, and systematically looting the neighbourhood. At the same time, a large number of Congolese military and police personnel suspected of involvement in the mutiny were arrested, and most were summarily executed on the nights of 14 and 15 May (Human Rights Watch, 2002, p. 1).

12 Deibert, 2014, p. 90.

13 Prunier, 2009, p. 298.

14 Deibert, 2014, p. 91.

15 Prunier, 2009, p. 309.

16 Ibid., p. 311.

17 Ibid., p. 313.

18 Trefon, 2011, p. 28.

19 Berwouts, 2007.

20 *Les cinq chantiers* – the five construction sites: Kabila promised in his campaign to make considerable improvements in five particular fields: infrastructure; employment; health; education; and water and electricity.

21 Trefon, 2011, p. 9.

22 Weiss and Nzongola-Ntalaja, 2013.

23 EurAc, 2008.

24 This paragraph is based on interviews with different people who lived and worked closely with Kabila for a time. For obvious reasons, they prefer to remain anonymous.

25 Vandaele, 2008.

26 My own interviews with diplomats of Congo's major western partners in 2007 and 2008.

27 Global Witness, 2011.

28 Van Reybrouck, 2014, p. 534.

29 Prunier, 2009, p. 320.

30 DDRRR involves disarmament, demobilization, repatriation, reintegration, and resettlement of foreign combatants. In Congo, it is often referred to as 'MONUC's programme of repatriation'.

31 Security sector reform is a core element of multidimensional peacekeeping and peacebuilding, essential for addressing the root causes of conflict and building the foundations of long-term peace and development. It involves reform of the army, the police and the juridical sector.

32 The paragraphs on the challenges of SSR in Congo are based on interviews I conducted with the people in charge of EUSEC (the European Mission in support of SSR in Congo), people working for the SSR programmes of different bilateral partners of Congo, Congolese officers and MPs.

33 Most of the information in the paragraphs on FDLR comes from interviews I conducted with two types of sources: firstly people working within the Congolese churches (Catholic as well as Protestant) to seek negotiated solutions for the FDLR problem, and secondly international researchers working on FDLR at grassroots level, including members of the Group of Experts on Congo and staff members of JMAC, MONUSCO's own intelligence service.

34 Prunier, 2008.

35 Ibid.

36 Ibid.

37 Interviews with JMAC, GoE members and Kabila's top negotiators on relations with the armed groups.

38 Prunier, 2008.

39 Ibid.

40 Stearns, 2012a, p. 39.

41 Prunier, 2008.

42 Ibid.

43 Ibid.

44 Stearns, 2012a, p. 39

45 Ibid., p. 39.

Chapter 4

1   Information received from members of the Group of Experts and staff members of JMAC.

2   UN Group of Experts, 2008.

3   Van Reybrouck, 2014, p. 522.

4   I was in Kivu the days *Umoja Wetu* started, with access to my confidential contacts within Kabila's and Kagame's inner circles. Information from these contacts feeds into these paragraphs.

5   Interviews with FARDC officers in Kivu.

6   Human Rights Watch, 2015a.

7   This issue will be elaborated further in the text below.

8   Hayman, 2011, pp. 118–131.

9   This letter was shown to me by a member of the Group of Experts.

10 Berwouts, 2013.

11 Peskin, 2011, pp. 173–183.

12 Tertsakian, 2011, pp. 210–222.

13 Berwouts, 2010b.

14 *Le Monde*, 27 August 2010.

Chapter 5

1   Interview with Jean-Claude Willame.
2   Human Rights Watch, 2009.
3   Evariste Boshab is an intellectual from the western Kasai province, who previously had an academic career and was one of the founding members of PPRD. Because of the fact that he always had a lot of power in the regime's machinery without having an electorate of his own, many people call him an apparatchik.
4   The Belgian filmmaker Thierry Michel made L'affaire Chebeya about the way the juridical system in Congo functioned or did not function.
5   HRW, 2012b.
6   Deibert, 2014, p. 178
7   HRW, 28 October 2011.
8   International Crisis Group, 2011.
9   EurAc's press release, 29 January 2012.
10 Carter Center, 2011.
11 Human Rights Watch, 2011.
12 Braeckman, 2012.
13 An interesting analysis of the technical, legal and political dimensions of the 2011 elections is Marcel Wetsh'okonda Koso, 2014. This work heavily influenced these paragraphs.
14 Bouvy and Lange, 2012.
15 Deibert, 2014, p. 202.
16 European Court of Auditors, 2013.

Chapter 6

1   Different people in the inner circle of Kabila's regime described Congo after Katumba Mwanke's death as a 'navire sans radar'.
2   The information in this paragraph comes from the UDPS MPs I talked to. They were frustrated that Tshisekedi forbade them to take up their mandates, since they considered that as the only way the party could fulfil its historical mission.
3   According to the members of the Group of Experts and the JMAC staff I talked to.
4   Interview with members of Kabila's team on eastern Congo.
5   Stearns, 2013.
6   Ibid., pp. 37–43.
7   Interview with one of Kabila's collaborators.
8   Ipis, 2012, pp. 5–10.
9   Stearns, 2012c.

10 UN Group of Experts, 2012.

11 Stearns, 2012a, pp. 46–48.

12 UN Group of Experts, 2012, pp. 7–15.

13 Ibid., pp. 16–18.

14 Ibid., pp. 19–20.

15 Interviews with UNHCR staff in Goma.

16 Human Rights Watch, 2013.

17 I could follow the negotiations almost in real time thanks to some diplomats who were in the room, and my permanent contacts with key negotiators of the DRC government.

18 Quote from the Peace, Security and Cooperation Framework Agreement for DRC and the region signed in Addis Ababa; February 2013.

19 International Crisis Group, 2014, pp. 3–4.

20 Information given to me by one of the top negotiators throughout the entire process.

21 Report from the European Court of Auditors, September 2013.

22 Autesserre, 2014, pp. 230–239.

23 I don't want to create the impression that Mamadou Ndala was a saint. People who worked with him, Congolese as well as expat military personnel, confirm that he was also actively involved in bad governance. But the people of North Kivu considered him an icon because of his role in M23's defeat. He embodied their hope for peace at that moment.

24 Jason Stearns interviewed by Voice of America on 30 December 2013.

25 Interviews with JMAC staff.

26 The Minister of Justice communicated immediately after his death that General Bahuma died of a stroke. Different intelligence sources confirmed to me that, in fact, he was killed.

27 UN Group of Experts, 2014.

28 This came back in many interviews with Congolese stakeholders from Beni-Butembo.

29 Information from Christoph Vogel, 2015.

30 International Crisis Group, 2014.

31 Mueller, 2015.

32 Vogel, 2014.

33 To give an idea: the budget for the twelve months between 1 July 2016 and 30 June 2017 is $1,235,723,100, according to the UN on http://www.un.org/en/peacekeeping/missions/monusco/facts.shtml. This figure does not take into account the salaries and operating costs of the staff delegated to MONUSCO by Congo's other multilateral and bilateral partners.

Chapter 7

1   BBC, 2013.
2   Interviews with expat interlocutors in Lubumbashi with strong connections to the north of the province and the Balubakat leadership.
3   This paragraph is based on interviews with long-term expats in Lubumbashi and people close to Kabila's inner circle.
4   The research for the following paragraphs was conducted for the Department for International Development (DfID) in April 2014. The aim was to map the uncertainties at the end of Kabila's second and constitutionally last mandate, and to draw some scenarios from that. Many insiders of the Congolese political landscape were interviewed for this study, as well as key figures from the international scene around it. The non-confidential parts of the study were published by my co-consultant Manya Riche and myself on African Arguments (Berwouts and Riche, 2014).
5   In January 2015 I started to work for the Stabilization Support Unit of MONUSCO. The paragraphs on the first six months of 2015 are based on experiences in that period, again with omission of the confidential parts.
6   Kyungu is a legendary leader in Katanga, an ex-governor of the province. He was one of the instigators of the ethnic violence against Luba migrant workers in Katanga, and their expulsion back to the Kasai.
7   The four other party leaders who together founded the G7 are José Endundu (PDC), Christophe Lutundula (MSDD), Charles Mwando Simba (UNADEF) and Danny Banza (ACO).
8   In August 2015.
9   Human Rights Watch, 2015b.
10 Berwouts, 2016.
11 Much of this is based on a study I conducted in March 2016 for DfID on the potential for street violence in Kinshasa. The results were published in a very reduced form by the Egmont Institute in June 2016 (Berwouts, 2016).
12 Berwouts, 2014.
13 Weiss and Nzongola-Ntalaja, 2013, p. 1.
14 This information comes from MP, opposition leader and MLC secretary general Eve Bazaiba, March 2016.

Conclusion

1   I conducted research for DfID into DRC's Evidence, Analysis and Coordination Programme (EACP), on behalf of Integrity Research and Consultancy, in March and April 2016. These paragraphs contain a summary of the conclusions.
2   International Crisis Group, 2016.
3   Vogel and Stearns, 2015.

4   Ibid.
5   Verweyen, 2016.
6   General Masunzu was transferred to Kamina in the military reshuffle of September 2014. Some people suggested that this was some sort of punishment for his role in the Mutarule massacre three months earlier, but this is very difficult to confirm.
7   Vogel and Stearns, 2015.
8   Vlassenroot and Berwouts, 2016.

REFERENCES

Autesserre, Séverine. 2012. 'Dangerous tales: dominant narratives on the Congo and their unintended consequences', *African Affairs*, Vol. 111 (443): 202-22.

Autesserre, Séverine. 2014. *Peaceland. Conflict Resolution and the Everyday Politics of International Intervention.* Cambridge and New York: Cambridge University Press.

BBC. 2013. 'DR Congo "repulses" TV, airport and army base attacks', 30 December.

Berwouts, Kris. 2001. *Congo.* Brussels: KIT Publishers, NOVIB.

Berwouts, Kris. 2007. EurAc Mission report, November, Brussels.

Berwouts, Kris. 2010. 'Rwanda face aux élections: les fissures dans le miroir'. EurAc Mission Report, Brussels.

Berwouts, Kris. 2013. 'In the shadow of the baobab: Kagame blows cold and hot on a third mandate', *African Arguments*, 18 March.

Berwouts, Kris. 2014. 'La Lucha – Goma's own brand of Indignados', *African Arguments*, 13 January.

Berwouts, Kris. 2016. 'The rise of the street. The population of Kinshasa as an unpredictable actor in the electoral process', *Africa Policy Brief*, Egmont Institute, June.

Berwouts, Kris and Riche, Manya. 2014. 'DRC elections: will Kabila stay or go? And many other questions on the road to 2016', *African Arguments*, 24 June.

Bouvy, Alexis and Lange, Maria. 2012. 'Ending the padlock. Towards a new vision of peace in the DRC', *International Alert*.

Braeckman, Colette. 2012. 'Le verdict des urnes ouvre le post-après-transition', *Le Soir*, 2 February.

Carter Center. 2011. 'DRC presidential election results lack credibility', 9 December.

Coolsaet, Rik. 2008. *Geschiedenis van de wereld van morgen.* Antwerp: Van Halewyck.

Deibert, Michael. 2014. *The Democratic Republic of the Congo: Between Hope and Despair.* London: Zed Books.

De Villers, Gauthier. 2009. *République démocratique du Congo. De la guerre aux élections.* Paris: Harmattan.

De Witte, Ludo. 2001. *The Assassination of Lumumba.* Brooklyn: Verso.

Enough Project. 2014. 'Deadly militia FDLR regrouping in Congo despite ticking clock'.

EurAc. 2008. 'Building democracy from the grass roots: Towards new leadership and good governance at local level'. Memorandum for the French Presidency of the EU, Brussels.

European Court of Auditors. 2013. 'EU support for governance in the Democratic Republic of the Congo'. ECA Special report 9.

Global Witness. 2011. *China and Congo. Friends in Need.* Global Witness, London.

Guevara, Ernesto Che. 2000. *The African Dream: The Diaries of the Revolutionary War in Congo.* New York: Grove.

Hayman, Rachel. 2011. 'Funding fraud? Donors and democracy in Rwanda', in Scott Strauss and Lars Waldorf, *Remaking Rwanda. State Building and Human Rights after Mass Violence.* Madison: University of Wisconsin Press.

Huggins, Chris. 2010. 'Land, power and identity. Roots of violent conflict in Eastern DRC'. Report, International Alert.

Human Rights Watch. 2002. 'Congo: war crimes in Kisangani', August. New York

Human Rights Watch. 2009. '"You will be punished". Attacks on civilians in Eastern Congo', December.

Human Rights Watch. 2011. 'DR Congo: candidates should not incite violence', 28 October.

Human Rights Watch. 2012. World Report.

Human Rights Watch. 2013. DR Congo: War Crimes by M23, Congolese Army. Response to Crisis in East Should Emphasize Justice.

Human Rights Watch. 2015. 'DRC, deadly crackdown on protests', 24 January.

International Alert. 2015. 'Beyond stabilization: understanding the conflict dynamics in North and South Kivu, Democratic Republic of Congo', February.

International Crisis Group. 2011. 'Congo, the electoral dilemma'.

International Crisis Group. 2014. 'Congo – Ending the status quo'. Africa briefing 107.

International Rescue Committee. 2007. 'Mortality in the Democratic Republic of Congo. An ongoing crisis', January.

IPIS. 2012. *Mapping Conflict Motives: M23.* IPIS, Antwerp.

Kennes, Erik. 2003. *Essai biographique sur Laurent Désiré KABILA.* Paris/Brussels: Harmattan/CEDAF.

Kyalangalilwa, Chrispin. 2014. 'Dozens killed in massacre in eastern Congo', Reuters, 7 June.

Lemarchand, René. 2001. 'The Democratic Republic of Congo: from collapse to potential reconstruction'. Centre of African Studies, University of Copenhagen.

Life and Peace Institute. 2012. 'Au delà des groups armés. Conflits locaux et connexions sous-régionales. L'example de Fizi et Uvira (Sud-Kivu, RDC)', Bakavu.

Mararo, Bucyalimwe. 1997. 'Land, power, and ethnic conflict in Masisi (Congo-Kinshasa), 1940s–1994', *International Journal of African Historical Studies*, 30, no. 3. 503-38.

Martens, Ludo. 1985. *Pierre Mulele ou la seconde vie de Patrice Lumumba*. Berchem: EPO.

Mathys, Gillian. 2014. 'People on the move. Frontiers, borders, mobility and history in the Lake Kivu region, 19th–20th century'. PhD thesis, University of Ghent.

Mueller, Timo. 2015. 'MONUSCO: Kobler's likely departure signals post-FIB era for peacekeeping in Congo', *African Arguments*, 25 February.

Newbury, David. 2009. *The Land beyond the Mists. Essays on Identity and Authority in Precolonial Congo and Rwanda*. Athens: Ohio University Press.

Peskin, Victor. 2011. 'Victor's justice revisited: Rwandan Patriotic Front crimes and the prosecutorial endgame', in Scott Strauss and Lars Waldorf (eds), *Remaking Rwanda: State Building and Human Rights after Mass Violence*. Madison: University of Wisconsin Press.

Prunier, Gérard. 2008. 'The eastern DR Congo: dynamics of conflict', Open Democracy, 18 November.

Prunier, Gérard. 2009. *From Genocide to Continental War. The 'Congolese' Conflict and the Crisis of Contemporary Africa*. London: Hurst.

Reyntjens, Filip. 2010. *La grande guerre africaine*. Paris: Les Belles Lettres.

Rotberg, Robert I. 2003. *State Failure and State Weakness in a Time of Terror*. Washington DC: Brookings Institution Press.

Stearns, Jason. 2012a. 'North Kivu. The background to conflict in North Kivu province of eastern Congo'. Rift Valley Institute & Usalama Project, Nairobi.

Stearns, Jason K. 2012b. *Dancing in the Glory of Monsters. The Collapse of Congo and the Great War of Africa*. New York: Public Affairs.

Stearns, Jason K. 2012c. From CNDP to M23. The Evolution of an Armed Movement in Eastern Congo. Rift Valley Institute, Nairobi.

Stearns, Jason. 2013. *Raia Mutomboki: The Flawed Peace Process in the DRC and the Birth of an Armed Franchise*. Rift Valley Institute, Nairobi.

Strauss, Scott and Waldorf, Lars (eds). 2011. *Remaking Rwanda: State Building and Human Rights after Mass Violence*. Madison: University of Wisconsin Press.

Tertsakian, Carina. 2011. '"All Rwandans are afraid of being arrested one day": Prisoners past, present and future', in Scott Strauss and Lars Waldorf (eds), *Remaking Rwanda: State Building and Human Rights after Mass Violence*. Madison: University of Wisconsin Press.

Remaking Rwanda: State Building and Human Rights after Mass Violence. Madison: University of Wisconsin Press.

Trefon, Theodore. 2011. *Congo Masquerade. The Political Culture of Aid Inefficiency and Reform*. London: Zed Books.

United Nations. 2010. Report of the Mapping Exercise documenting the most serious violations of human rights and international humanitarian law committed within the territory of the Democratic Republic of the Congo between March 1993 and June 2003, August.

UN Group of Experts. 2008. Final report of the Group of Experts on the Democratic Republic of Congo. United Nations Security Council, S/2008/773.

UN Group of Experts. 2012: Final report of the Group of Experts on the Democratic Republic of Congo. United Nations Security Council.

UN Group of Experts. 2014: Final report of the Group of Experts on the Democratic Republic of Congo. United Nations Security Council.

Van Reybrouck, David. 2014. *Congo. The Epic History of a People*. New York: Harper Collins.

Vandaele, John. 2008. 'Het Congolese roofdier, Mozes in Katanga en de Chinezen', Mo Magazine, February.

Vansina, Jan. 1982. 'Mwasi's trials', *Daedalus*, Vol. 111, No. 2. 49-70

Verweyen, Judith. 2016. 'Stable instability: political settlements and armed groups in the Congo'. Rift Valley Institute, Usalama Project, Nairobi.

Vlassenroot, Koen. 2013. *South Kivu: Identity, Territory, and Power in the Eastern Congo*. Rift Valley Institute.

Vlassenroot, Koen and Berwouts, Kris. 2016. 'Congo's political crisis after 19 December', *African Arguments*, 21 December.

Vogel, Christoph. 2014. 'Islands of instability or swamps of insecurity: MONUSCO's intervention brigade and the danger of emerging security voids in eastern Congo'. Africa Policy Brief, Egmont Institute, February.

Vogel, Christoph and Stearns, Jason, 2015. *The Landscape of the Armed Groups*. Congo Research Group, Center on International Cooperation, New York.

Weiss, Herbert F. and Nzongola-Ntalaja, Georges. 2013. 'Decentralization and the DRC – an overview'. Document prepared for the DRC Affinity Group, January.

Wetsh'okonda Koso, Marcel. 2014. *Le pari du respect de la vérité des urnes en Afrique.* [11.11.11, Brussels. 7]

Willame, Jean-Claude. 1997. *Banayarwanda et Banyamulenge. Violences ethniques et gestion de l'identitaire au Kivu*. Brussels: Cahiers Africains.

Willame, Jean-Claude. 2007. *Les 'faiseurs de paix' au Congo. Gestion d'une crise internationale dans un État sous tutelle*. Paris/Bruxelles: GRIP/Editions Complexe.

INDEX